JEFF PIERCE

R£7-95
8H

The Incarnation

CU00951946

This book gathers together essays, published and unpublished, in which Brian Hebblethwaite explores and defends
the Christian doctrine of the Incarnation against its modern
critics. He shows what would be lost from the Christian
religion if non-incarnational Christology (a way of understanding Jesus Christ without belief in his divinity) were to be
adopted by the Christian churches. He begins by examining
some of the problems raised by this challenge to traditional
doctrine, considers the contribution of Austin Farrer to
Christology, and goes on to analyse the recent trend towards
unitarianism in contemporary theology.

In a new, concluding essay, Canon Hebblethwaite answers
criticisms of his contribution to the current debate on the
Incarnation.

THE INCARNATION

Collected Essays in Christology

BRIAN HEBBLETHWAITE

*Fellow and Dean of Chapel in Queens' College
Cambridge and University Lecturer in Divinity*

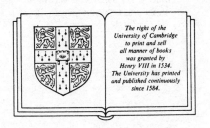

The right of the
University of Cambridge
to print and sell
all manner of books
was granted by
Henry VIII in 1534.
The University has printed
and published continuously
since 1584.

CAMBRIDGE UNIVERSITY PRESS

Cambridge

*London   New York   New Rochelle
Melbourne   Sydney*

Published by the Press Syndicate of the University of Cambridge
The Pitt Building, Trumpington Street, Cambridge CB2 1RP
32 East 57th Street, New York, NY 10022, USA
10 Stamford Road, Oakleigh, Melbourne 3166, Australia

First published 1987

Printed in Great Britain at
the University Press, Cambridge

British Library cataloguing in publication data
Hebblethwaite, Brian
The Incarnation: collected essays in
Christology.
1. Incarnation
I. Title
232′.1 BT220

Library of Congress cataloguing in publication data
Hebblethwaite, Brian.
The Incarnation: collected essays in Christology.
Bibliography.
1. Incarnation. 2. Jesus Christ – Person and
offices. I. Title.
BT220.H35 1987 232′.1 87–33351

ISBN 0 521 33352 0 hard covers
ISBN 0 521 33640 6 paperback

Contents

Contents

Preface

A decade after the publication of *The Myth of God Incarnate*, I have decided to gather together my various articles and papers on Christology, for the most part written in response to that collection. Many people would no doubt say that the debate has now moved on from the doctrine of the Person of Christ to the doctrine of God. My colleague, Don Cupitt, one of the contributors to *The Myth*, has presented, in more recent years, a much more radical and far-reaching programme of 'demythologising' all God-talk and treating all religious language as simply expressive of certain moral and spiritual commitments alone. I am responding to this more radical view elsewhere; but I want to return here to Christology because in the earlier debate there can be discerned a much more pervasive trend in Christian theology than in the more recent extreme position of Don Cupitt. Non-incarnational Christology represents a much more serious threat to the faith of the Christian Church than does Cupitt's virtual atheism just because there is a greater likelihood of the former coming to prevail than the latter. Non-incarnational Christology is an attractive option for Christian believers who hold a strong belief in the reality of God, but who feel the force of the intellectual and moral objections to the idea of the divinity of Jesus Christ. In particular the exigencies of inter-faith dialogue have underlined the religious attractiveness of non-incarnational Christology. Yet I believe it to be false and have tried to say in these various pieces why I believe it to be false.

Preface

Chapters 1 and 2 were published in *Theology* for March and July 1977, the former, therefore, anticipating *The Myth of God Incarnate* by a few months, although the trends moving in the direction of that collection were already clearly visible. Chapter 3 was published in *The Truth of God Incarnate*, edited by Michael Green (Hodder and Stoughton 1977), a somewhat over-hasty response to the *Myth* book. Chapters 4 and 5 appeared in *Incarnation and Myth: The Debate Continued*, edited by Michael Goulder (SCM Press 1979), a volume stemming from a 'seven-a-side' debate held in Birmingham University in 1978. Chapter 6, written for a conference of the Anglican and German Evangelical Churches in Kloster Loccum, West Germany, in 1978, was published in the *Scottish Journal of Theology* for April 1980. Chapters 7 and 8 have not been published before. They were delivered as papers to a conference on Catholic Renewal in Oxford in 1980. Chapter 9 was published in *New Fire* for Winter 1977 and reflects my longstanding debt to the philosophical theology of Austin Farrer. Chapter 10 was published, under the title 'Recent British Theology' in *One God in Trinity*, edited by Peter Toon and James D. Spiceland (Samuel Bagster 1980). Chapter 11 was published in the Festschrift for my teacher, Donald MacKinnon, *The Philosophical Frontiers of Christian Theology*, edited by Brian Hebblethwaite and Stewart Sutherland (CUP 1982). I have taken the opportunity to revise these pieces a little, but I am grateful to the publishers and editors of the journals and collections in question for permission to reprint.

I have added, as Chapter 12, a new essay on Christology, responding to various criticisms of my views and reflecting further on the centrality of the doctrine of the Incarnation in Christianity.

1

Incarnation – the essence of Christianity?

> My song is love unknown,
>   My Saviour's love to me,
> Love to the loveless shown,
>   That they might lovely be.
> O who am I
>   That for my sake
>   My Lord should take
> Frail flesh and die?

This popular Passiontide hymn expresses very simply a characteristic Christian devotional response to the Incarnation. I take it that the writer meant by the first line not that this love *remains* unknown, but that, prior to the taking of frail flesh, it *was* (relatively speaking) unknown. *Now*, by contrast, the saving action of incarnation – to the point of crucifixion – has revealed that previously unknown love, and the effect of this revelation is to be the transformation of the loveless into the lovely.

There can be no doubt that the doctrine of the Incarnation has been taken during the bulk of Christian history to constitute the very heart of Christianity. Hammered out over five centuries of passionate debate, enshrined in the classical Christian creeds, explored and articulated in the great systematic theologies, the doctrine expresses, so far as human words permit, the central belief of Christians that God himself, without ceasing to be God, has come amongst us, not just in but *as* a particular man, at a particular time and place. The human life lived and the death died have been held quite

1

literally to *be* the human life and death of God himself in one of the modes of his own eternal being. Jesus Christ, it has been firmly held, was truly God as well as being truly man. As we have seen, this belief is not only expressed in the doctrine of the Incarnation, but also in countless hymns and devotional rites that belong to the very stuff of living Christianity, not to mention the art and sculpture which it has inspired down the centuries.

This extraordinary doctrine has, nevertheless, been widely questioned since the Enlightenment and the rise of modern science, not only from without but from within the Christian Church. Recently, in England, there has been a spate of books and articles criticising traditional incarnational Christology as unintelligible and defending a non-incarnational Christology as quite sufficient to do justice to the figure of Jesus and to what God did in and through him. I wish to discuss this present phase of the debate, not because there is anything particularly original in current non-incarnational Christology in England (as opposed to that of Ernst Troeltsch, for example, in the early years of this century in Germany), but because the issues are being presented now with great simplicity and clarity, and this makes for easier dialogue. Examples of the writings which I have in mind are Norman Pittenger's *Christology Reconsidered*, John Robinson's *The Human Face of God*, Maurice Wiles' *The Remaking of Christian Doctrine*, John Hick's *God and the Universe of Faiths*, and an article by Don Cupitt, now reprinted in *The Leap of Reason*, called 'The Finality of Christ'.[1]

Two claims stand out as typical of these approaches to Christology. On the one hand, it is asserted that we cannot accept the old formulations since it is simply incoherent, self-contradictory, to speak of one who is both God and man; and on the other hand, it is urged that what the old formulations were trying to express about the significance of Jesus for us can be rescued from its involvement in this incoherence and expressed more simply and more adequately by speaking of

God's acts in and through the man Jesus, or of Jesus' peculiar, indeed unique, openness to the divine Spirit. I wish to refute both these claims, and, in doing so, to bring out their interconnection.

My colleague, Don Cupitt, writes: 'The eternal God, and a historical man, are two beings of quite different ontological status. It is simply unintelligible to declare them identical.' Similarly, John Hick has repeated Spinoza's comment that talk of one who is both God and man is like talk of a square circle. Both writers are so convinced that a literal doctrine of Incarnation *cannot* be true, that they try to represent this as a logical impossibility. Yet as soon as we examine these assertions it becomes clear that no case whatsoever has actually been made out for the conclusion that incarnation-talk is self-contradictory. What, after all, is the basis for comparing talk of one who is both God and man to talk of a square circle? Certainly a square circle is a contradiction in terms. The terms 'square' and 'circle' are precisely defined terms, and their logical incompatibility is obvious from the definitions. But 'God' and 'man' are far from being such tightly defined concepts. It is difficult enough to suppose that we have a full and adequate grasp of what is is to be a human being. We certainly have no such grasp of the divine nature. Who are we to say that the essence of God is such as to rule out the possibility of his making himself present in the created world as a human being, while in no way ceasing to be the God he ever is? A similar point can be made in respect of Cupitt's remarks. Certainly the eternal God and a historical man are beings of different ontological status. But the claim of the Christian tradition has been that the ontology of God is such as to permit the infinite source of all created being to come amongst us as a man. Again, who are we to say that the ontological status of God is such as to render this logically impossible? Modern theologians are much too ready to cry 'contradiction'. As Ninian Smart has wisely observed in

3

another context: 'It is doubtful whether the God–manhood of Christ is a strict contradiction, e.g., Christ was for a time in Galilee while God is from eternity in Heaven, and Christ is God: does this constitute a contradiction? Only if Heaven and Galilee are both places in the same sense of "place".'[2]

We shall see in a moment *why* the writers in question feel bound to press their case so far as to accuse the doctrine of the Incarnation of self-contradiction. For the moment we note the baselessness of this accusation and turn to their other claim, namely that everything which the tradition has claimed regarding the revelatory and salvific significance of Jesus Christ can be retained without the belief that he was God as well as man. I should like to test this claim by describing two features in incarnational Christology which seem to me to be of great profundity, and asking whether non-incarnational Christology can ever hope to give us such religiously significant insights into the ways of God with man.

The first feature of the traditional belief to which I should like to draw attention is its insistence on the direct personal encounter between God and man made possible by the Son of God's coming amongst us as one of us. Certainly God's dealings with man prior to the Incarnation and through other religious traditions can be construed as personal. Spirituality, prophetic inspiration, mystical experience, can all be construed in personal terms, as they are in all the great religions of Semitic origin, and indeed in many of the Eastern faiths as well. But the Incarnation represents a new and much more direct, face-to-face way of personal encounter this side of the divide between infinite and finite than is envisaged in the modes of inspiration or illumination. Certainly those modes imply an immanent, not just a transcendent God, but the manner of the divine presence in the world is surely differently conceived when it is supposed that God comes face to face with us as another human being. The difference is brought out beautifully by Søren Kierkegaard in *Philosophical Fragments* by means of his parable

4

of the king and the humble maiden. The king can only win the maiden's love if he lays aside his royal robes and woos her as an ordinary man, person to person, in her own village. There are two points here. The king must do this himself; it is no use just sending a messenger. Secondly, he must do so in a way which does not overwhelm the humble girl by the panoply of royalty. Of course, this is only a parable for the incarnation, and it fails at many points, especially in so far as the king's 'condescension' involves only a change of clothes. But the main point stands, that there is a difference between God's making himself known indirectly through the awe-inspiring medium of 'the holy' or through a prophet, and God's coming himself incognito, and winning a purely personal response. To suppose that God's act in or presence to the man Jesus is simply a higher example of the kind of inspiration or illumination to be found elsewhere in the history of religions and thus of supreme exemplary significance for our own 'God-consciousness' is not to reinterpret the Christian tradition. It is to lose the peculiarly Christian contribution, namely that experience of God can now take a much more direct and personal form, since God himself has humbled himself and come among us as one of us.

My second test for non-incarnational Christology's adequacy concerns the way in which Christianity claims to meet the problem of evil. One of its most profound claims is that God in Christ subjected *himself* to the world's evil at its most harsh and cruel, and by so doing both revealed his love and accepted responsibility for the suffering entailed by the creation of an organic self-reproducing world of sentient and free persons. There is a profoundly moral insight here. The divine love and forgiveness are shown most clearly in the lengths to which our God is prepared to go to win the love of the loveless 'that they might lovely be'. These things cannot be done through a representative. No doubt it is possible to express sympathy and sorrow indirectly through someone else. But there is all the difference in the world between the sending of condolences and actually bearing the brunt of the suffering oneself. The point about God's taking responsibility for the world's evil, moreover, depends wholly on the Incarnation. In no way can he be supposed to take responsibility for the world's ills through the suffering of a human representative.

By both these tests, then, a non-incarnational Christology fails. The moral and religious significance of Christ's life and death depends on his being God in person. But now, perhaps, we see the reason why our christological revisionists have to press their case to the point of crying contradiction. The moral and religious sense which I have claimed to discern in the doctrine of the Incarnation depends, of course, on that doctrine making sense. If the notion of God made man is a nonsense, then any purported moral and religious significance in the notion must be illusory. If in the nature of the case God's presence in the world can take no deeper form than that of inspiration or illumination, then it is folly to suggest or claim anything more. God is as fully present in and to the inspired prophet Jesus of Nazareth as it is logically possible for God to be present in and to a man. But if, on the contrary, something more is logically possible, then non-incarnational Christology is on pretty shaky ground. If God might have become man, but did not, then the reduced claims for what God has done in Christ fail to satisfy. But, as we have seen, the case for holding the notion of one who is both God and man to be self-contradictory has not been made out. So the moral and religious sense which we can come to see in the belief that the Cross of Christ is God's Cross in our world is bound to make the non-incarnational Christologies appear inadequate and a pale shadow of orthodox Christian doctrine.

Many writers have spoken of the appropriateness of the Incarnation. Not that we could have predicted it very easily, although there are significant intimations of the notion elsewhere in the history of religions. But given the life, death and resurrection of Jesus Christ and the experience of the gift of the Spirit, the resultant doctrine of the Incarnation evokes our immediate recognition of its appropriateness. Many creative innovations in religion and ethics have this curious ability at once to introduce something new and to make us say, yes, it could not have been otherwise.

Of all the writers I mention at the beginning, John Hick is the one who has come up with the most persuasive reason for demythologising the Incarnation. Only by so doing, on Hick's view, can one make moral and religious sense of the relation between the developing world religions as different and equally valid channels of the saving encounter between God and man – man, that is, in his different historical and cultural traditions. I say that this global ecumenism makes moral and religious sense, but one cannot proceed in an *a priori* manner in these matters. One has actually to look at the beliefs and doctrines of the religions as they have emerged, and it is very hard to see that the specifically Christian claims can really be made to fit this pattern. Moreover I have to set against the appealing nature of Hick's relativistic hypothesis the moral and religious sense of the doctrine of the Incarnation as I have tried to expound it above. This, I urged, depends on our recognising in the man Jesus God himself come amongst us to make himself known in personal encounter and to take the brunt of the world's evil upon himself. This, one realises, could only be done at the cost of introducing an asymmetry into the history of religions. (The notion of many incarnations cannot carry the same force, if God is one, and a particular man can *be* God to us in a fully human personal context. To suppose that God might have several human faces is to lose the real personal revelatory significance of the Incarnation.)[3] Consequently, whatever knowledge and experience of God is mediated to our Jewish, Muslim, Hindu and Buddhist friends by their respective traditions – and it is a mistake to depreciate that knowledge and experience –

the Christian cannot withdraw his invitation to them and to all men to see in Jesus Christ something more, and something necessarily unique.

It is interesting to note that Hick has to reinforce his relativistic view by going on to urge that the notion of one who is both God and man is self-contradictory. But this contradiction was only 'discovered' after he had already adopted the relativistic view of *God and the Universe of Faiths* on other grounds. Such a belated logical discovery does not inspire confidence. I recall the discussion of these topics at the Society for the Study of Theology at Lancaster some years ago, when Ninian Smart made the nice point that he could not see why Professor Hick was so sure that 'God' and 'man' were incompatible, when he was equally sure that the religions' different concepts of God as 'personal' and 'impersonal' were ultimately compatible. The point is worth pondering. One might well think that the latter conjunction has more in common with a 'square circle' than the former.

I should like to turn to the recent article by Harry Williams in *Theology* for January 1976. That article seems to me to be totally misconceived. It begins with the false premise that 'it is difficult for us not to assume that in the doctrine of the incarnation we have some sort of literal description or representational picture'. We assume nothing of the kind. The statement that God reveals himself and his forgiving love by coming amongst us as one of us and bearing the brunt of the world's evil himself is in no sense a symbolic, picturing or representational statement. No doubt it assumes some personal model in respect of its subject, 'God', but the statement itself remains quite agnostic about the ontological possibilities of God's self-manifestation or the *manner* of his making himself present in our midst. Certainly there *are* ways of picturing the incarnation – the kenotic model, for instance, or Kierkegaard's model of the king and the humble maiden – and they are admittedly highly anthropomorphic. No doubt, as Williams suggests, we need a mutually qualifying plurality of models of the Incarnation. But the point is that these are models of the Incarnation. Incarnation is not itself one of the models. Rather it is what is being pictured in these various inadequate ways.

Treating 'incarnation' as itself a model leads Williams at once into the 'square circle' dilemma, which, as we have seen, has no real basis. It is precisely because we are *not* operating with a readily available concept or picture of God, but pointing away from our own pictures to an infinite transcendent reality much greater than anything we can think or say that we can consider the possibility that God is literally such as to be able, without ceasing to be God, to make himself known in human form.

Having started off on the wrong foot, Williams goes on to make confusion worse confounded by offering as one among many models a psychological model, in which the split between the knowing subject and the known object is overcome. But the irrelevance of this model becomes apparent only too soon; for we find that Williams is not really offering this as a model for the Incarnation at all, but rather for the relation between God and man as such. But that is a different subject. Maybe the psychological model might help us with a doctrine of the Spirit, but, as we have seen above, the notion of the divine inspiration of a human prophet cannot do the same job as the doctrine of the Incarnation. The moral and religious force of Jesus' life and death depends on his *being* God incarnate. And if Williams is to press the argument the other way and suggest through his psychological model that we are all God incarnate, well, that is an interesting piece of theosophy, but it has little to do with Christian doctrine.

The suggestion that, of all the human beings who have trod the earth, Jesus of Nazareth alone was divine is undoubtedly an extraordinary suggestion. It is not surprising that in our relativistic and secular age even Christians find it hard to swallow. But then belief in God is an extraordinary belief for the scientific or historicist mind. If we are seriously to suppose that there is a transcendent source of being and value, an infinite Creator on whom this whole evolving world and the whole history of man depend, then we cannot refrain from taking seriously the different possible ways of construing the self-revelation of God to man that have emerged from the history of religions. One such way is to see that revelation as focused in a unique personal presence of God as a particular man at a particular time and place within the historical process. I have said something of the moral and religious force of such a view. There is a great deal more that could be said. Moreover the question of the historical evidence for reading things this way has not been examined here, and much depends on the plausibility of that case. But of one thing I am quite certain – that the doctrine of the Incarnation represents the peculiarly Christian contribution to the religions' ways of speaking of God's dealings with man and man's experience and knowledge of God.

2

Perichoresis – reflections on the doctrine of the Trinity

> Can poets (can men in television)
>   Be saved? It is not easy
> To believe in unknowable justice
>   Or pray in the name of a love
> Whose name one's forgotten: libera
>   Me, libera C (dear C)
> And all poor s–o–b's who never
>   Do anything properly, spare
> Us in the youngest day, when all are
>   Shaken awake, facts are facts
> (And I shall know exactly what happened
>   Today between noon and three)
> That we, too, may come to the picnic
>   With nothing to hide, join the dance
> As it moves in perichoresis
>   Turns about the abiding tree.

This is the final stanza in W. H. Auden's *Compline*, one of the poems that make up his *Horae Canonicae*. It is a striking fact that the technical theological term 'perichoresis' can appear with such effect in a modern poem. It may take a little homework to enable the reader to appreciate its effectiveness; but there can be no doubt that it invests the poem's conclusion with great imaginative force.

To save the homework, let me explain that the term 'perichoresis', from the Greek for 'encircling' or 'encompassing', acquired the technical sense in theology of 'mutual interpenetration'. Taken over from its less happy usage in

11

Christology into trinitarian theology, it was used by Pseudo-Cyril and John of Damascus to refer to the co-inherence of the three persons in the one eternal God. In G. L. Prestige's words, 'it stands as a monument of inspired Christian rationalism'.[1] One might add that in Auden's poem it becomes also a focus of inspired Christian imagination.

How strange, then, that in theology itself such words have lost their power! Not only has the Christian mind in general ceased to register the significance of the technical terms of orthodox trinitarian theology, but many theologians themselves now recommend us to jettison such terms and indeed the doctrine of the Trinity itself as part of the outworn lumber of the Christian past. Thus Maurice Wiles writes in his essay in *Christian Believing*: 'I cannot with integrity say that I believe God to be one in three persons.'[2]

Yet in the same essay Wiles correctly points out that 'Christian faith has been especially distinguished from other faiths by the trinitarian character of its affirmations about God'. As Peter Geach says in *God and the Soul*, the missionaries who first evangelised England taught the English not to apply the word 'God' any more to Woden, Thor and other imaginary beings, but solely to the Blessed Trinity.[3] In a more robust age, Calvin could say: 'For God so proclaims himself the sole God as to offer himself to be contemplated clearly in three persons. Unless we grasp these, only the bare and empty name of God flits about in our brains, to the exclusion of the true God.'[4] Admittedly we are disposed to think more charitably these days of other faiths (after all we are in dialogue with members of the world religions, not with worshippers of Thor), and it is far from clear that our specifically Christian recognition of God's trinitarian nature need necessarily lead us to disparage the spirituality and insight fostered in other faiths. It is possible to hold at the same time that in many different contexts and traditions men and women have grasped something of the invisible nature of

God, and also that God has revealed himself much more fully, through the Incarnation of his Son and the gift of his Spirit, as none other than the Blessed Trinity.

Certainly, where trinitarian faith is being abandoned it seems that the characterisation of God which remains is more than somewhat vague. Ernst Troeltsch, whose increasing consciousness of the historical relativity of all religious traditions led him to forsake his earlier conviction of the 'absoluteness' of Christianity, observes, in a dithyrambic passage in his last lecture, which was to be given in Oxford in 1923: 'All religion has thus a common goal in the Unknown, the Future, perchance in the Beyond.'[5] Possibly so, but we are not much the wiser for this insight. As Auden says, 'it is not easy to pray in the name of a love whose name one's forgotten'. But it needs to be stressed against Troeltsch and his modern followers that, despite the difficulty of identifying divine revelation amidst the welter of religious revelation-claims, we cannot just rule out the possibility of genuine disclosure from the side of God.

The bulk of my remarks will be concerned with the claim that in Christ and through the gift of the Spirit, God has revealed himself as the Blessed Trinity, and that the doctrine of Trinity is our human attempt, within the limitations of finite experience and human language, to state the content of that revelation. But first I should like to ask whether there are any purely rational considerations, irrespective of specifically Christian revelation, that might point to the idea of relation in God, and drive us to qualify the notion of absolute and undifferentiated monotheism, which seems to be the natural resting place alike of the religious and of the metaphysical mind.

In the same article from which I have already quoted, Wiles says: 'I certainly believe that there is one God whose being is infinitely rich and complex, but . . .'. This is an example of the vagueness and generality to which one tends to be driven when one becomes convinced of the cultural and

historical relativity of all traditions and formulations. But it
is worth asking why Wiles is prepared to say even this and
moreover to tell us that 'certainly' he believes this. Is it a
residual conviction, despite the relativities, that God has
revealed himself to be 'infinitely rich and complex', or is it a
purely rational belief, based on religious and metaphysical
dissatisfaction with the notion of an undifferentiated absolute? It could be the latter. For there are indeed considerations which make for such dissatisfaction, at least within the
framework of personal theism as opposed to impersonal
monism. If personal analogies are held to yield some insight
into the divine nature (perhaps because man is supposed to be
made in the image of God), then there can be no doubt that
the model of a single individual person does create difficulties
for theistic belief. It presents us with a picture of one who,
despite his infinite attributes, is unable to enjoy the excellence
of personal relation unless he first create an object for his love.
Monotheistic faiths have not favoured the idea that creation
is necessary to God, but short of postulating personal relation
in God, it is difficult to see how they can avoid it. There does
seem to be something of an impasse here for Judaism and
Islam. Hinduism, at least in its more philosophical forms,
avoids this problem by refusing to push the personal analogies
right back into the absolute itself. The personal gods of Hindu
devotional religion are held by the philosophers to be per-
sonifications at a lower level of reality of the one absolute
being, beyond all attributes. (Hence, incidentally, the so-
called Hindu Trinity of Brahma, Vishnu and Siva is no real
analogue for the Christian Trinity.) This rational and
religious aporia in the very concept of pure monotheism is, of
course, not sufficient to suggest trinitarian belief. The argument contains no indication of the number of relations to be
postulated, and provides very little in the way of a positive
idea of an internally differentiated deity. It may suggest
'richness and complexity' in God, but remains extremely

vague. Nevertheless, it does, I believe, give a point of contact
– an *Anknüpfungspunkt* – for trinitarian theology.

Trinitarian theology proper appeals to revelation. It is, as
Leonard Hodgson put it,

> the product of rational reflection on those particular manifestations
> of the divine activity which centre in the birth, ministry, crucifix-
> ion, resurrection and ascension of Jesus Christ and the gift of the
> Holy Spirit to the Church . . . It could not have been discovered
> without the occurrence of those events, which drove human reason
> to see that they required a trinitarian God for their cause.[6]

Wiles, in an earlier article, now reprinted in *Working Papers in
Doctrine*, takes exception to this approach of Hodgson on the
grounds that the different divine activities do not in fact compel us to postulate a trinitarian God. On the contrary, the
Fathers were quite unable to distribute the divine activities
amongst the persons of the Trinity severally, and soon came
to the very different conclusion summed up in the Latin tag:
opera Trinitatis ad extra sunt indivisa.[7] This point is well made
and documented, but it in no way meets Hodgson's argument; for Hodgson was not concerned to trace three sorts of
divine activity in the world and ascribe them to three different
sources or 'persons' in God. Rather he was concerned to
make the very different point that God's gift of himself to man
takes two radically different forms in the Incarnation and in
the outpouring of the Spirit, and that, despite the involvement of the whole Godhead in these two modes of self-
presentation within the world, nevertheless their essentially
relational nature discloses to us the fact that God exists in his
own being as the Blessed Trinity. This is the argument I wish
to explore.

The starting-point of the argument is that the Incarnation
and particularly the relation between the incarnate one and
his heavenly Father reveal and portray to us in terms we can
readily understand the eternal relation of love given and love
received within the deity. Now the doctrine of the Incarnation

15

is itself under attack – not surprisingly, by the same people who would have us demythologise the Trinity – and in the previous chapter I tried to say something in its defence. But for present purposes I simply wish to point out that it was conviction of the divinity of Christ that in the first place necessitated the postulation of real relations in God. For if the language and devotion suitable to God were now being applied to the risen Christ, then clearly the implication was that God is sufficiently 'rich and complex' in his own being to be able, without ceasing to be God, to make himself personally present in human history as a man, and to relate himself to himself in the manner in which we read of Jesus' prayers to the Father. Precisely that relation was the revealed form of the eternal personal relation subsisting within the Godhead. Only in such terms can the divinity of Christ be understood.

This is not a frivolous argument. The profundities of religious insight to which it gives rise are well illustrated in the very different works of Hans Urs von Balthasar and Jürgen Moltmann, to mention only two modern theologians. As I argued in the first chapter, it shows us God's way of meeting evil at a level quite unattainable by any other kind of Christology. In a nutshell, the way in which we see in Jesus Christ the inner differentiations of deity revealed and enacted not only for our illumination but for our salvation, is the mainspring of the doctrine of the Trinity.

But it will not have escaped notice that my argument so far is most naturally taken as an argument not for trinitarian, but for binitarian belief. One recalls the treatment of this theme by Austin Farrer in *Saving Belief*, where he says quite categorically that 'the revealed parable of the Godhead is a story about two characters, Father and Son', and 'the Trinity is not a society of three, but a society of two'.[8] Admittedly he goes on to indicate where the human parable breaks down and how we are driven to postulate more 'richness and complexity' (to return to Wiles' phrase) in the case of God than in the human case of a relation between two people. It is this step, the step beyond binitarian to trinitarian belief, that is the most difficult and problematic aspect of the doctrine of the Trinity.

Is this a necessary step, and, if so, why? At first sight, when we go on to consider the gift of the Spirit, it does not seem necessary to postulate a further relation in God. It seems enough to be able to speak of the Spirit of God or of the Spirit of Christ (it is a consequence of incarnational belief that the early Christians and we can speak indifferently of either) at work in the world, in the Church and in our hearts. There are some indications, however, that such talk misses what is characteristically Christian in Christian talk of the Spirit, as opposed to language about the divine spirit current in other religions including Judaism. For the experience of inspiration and possession of which the early Christians speak, and which came to shape the liturgical expression of the Christian Church, were, it seems, of a very special kind. It was not simply that Christians experienced 'power from on high'. Consider what Paul writes about the Spirit in Romans 8. In the cry 'Abba! Father', he says, 'the Spirit of God joins with our spirit in testifying that we are God's children' and 'We do not know how we ought to pray, but through our inarticulate groans, the Spirit himself is pleading for us, and God, who searches our inmost being, knows what the Spirit means, because he pleads for God's people in God's own way.' I am not trying to prove anything just by quoting scripture. All I am suggesting is that the experience reflected in the kind of language used in Romans 8 seems to consist in a sense of being caught up, when our prayer falters, into God's own interior dialogue. Is there not here, after all, another indication of relation in God? The way in which our prayers are caught up into God's own self-address reveals the reality of a further internal relation in the deity.

Some theologians, however, would want to argue that this

is not a different relation from that disclosed in the Incarnation. The assimilation can take one of two forms. Either the relation between God and Jesus is assimilated to that between the Spirit and ourselves and so we get a 'spirit' Christology such as Professor Lampe explored in his Bampton Lectures,[9] or the latter relation is assimilated to the former, as in Harry Williams' talk of incarnation as the relation between God and man in general.[10]

Neither proposal, in my view, will work. I spoke above of the 'radically different forms' of God's gift of himself to man in the Incarnation and in the outpouring of the Spirit. The reason for this is precisely the special and unique way in which the Christian tradition has found itself driven to speak of Jesus as *being* divine. I tried to expound this in the first chapter, and obviously the arguments there applied to the case of Jesus cannot apply to our own case. Once we start speaking of ourselves in any sense as *being* God, we have lost touch with Christianity. Not even Eastern Orthodox talk of 'divinisation' should be taken to blur the Creator–creature distinction, where we are concerned.

The matter is not at all easy to articulate, however. If we cannot conflate the God–God relation revealed in the love of the incarnate one for his heavenly Father with the God–God relation revealed in the way the Spirit takes up our prayers and worship into God's own self-address, nevertheless the latter relation is both presupposed by and supremely evident in the former, and itself has to be pressed back into the essential Trinity. The Father indwells the Son by his Spirit. As Farrer says, it is at this point that the human parable of love between two people breaks down.

Nevertheless the revelation of love given and love received within the deity has its locus in the Incarnation, not in the gift of the Spirit. It is Christ who shows us that God is love, and he does this by his prayers to the Father as much as by his qualities and his deeds. We see in him that God is not only loving towards his creatures but exists in his own eternal and infinite being in the relationship of love. The further 'richness and complexity' revealed in the Spirit's indwelling in Christ and derivatively in his assumption of our prayer and worship cannot be thought of as exactly symmetrical with the primary personal relation of love between the Father and the Son. Nor is the experience of possession by the Spirit an independent basis for trinitarian reflection. Without the revelation of God's nature in Christ, we would be unlikely to construe the activity of the Spirit in these relational terms. We may be driven to postulate two different relations within the Godhead and hence three 'persons' – to use the technical term – but the social analogy remains rooted in the relation of Jesus to his heavenly Father.

But if there are pressures which take us beyond a binitarian into a trinitarian theology, why do we stop there? Why not postulate further relations still within the infinite being of God? The answer is that the self-revelation of God in the Incarnation and the gift of the Spirit does not imply any more internal relations. Rationally speaking, we might speculate further; but God has revealed himself as the Blessed Trinity.

One further point needs to be made. I have made no use of the psychological analogy, common in trinitarian thinking from Augustine to Lonergan. In fact I think it much less helpful in our attempts to explain the characteristic Christian belief that God is three in one. It is as ambiguous in trinitarian theology as the attempts criticised by Wiles and others to find and distribute threefold patterns of activity in God's dealings with his creation. I have relied here on the social analogy, even if, following Farrer, I have expressed doubts about thinking in terms of a society of three. But what about the common accusation that the social analogy inevitably leads us into tritheism (or perhaps in our case bitheism)? This accusation has no substance. What, after all, would it be to believe in three or two gods? It would be to believe in a number of finite supernatural beings related externally, each existing in a sphere exclusive of the other or others. The social analogy postulates nothing of the kind, and could only be thought to do so by those endowed with excessive literal-mindedness. The social analogy is an *analogy*. It invites us to consider the possibility that the 'infinite richness and complexity' of the one God embraces the fullness of love given and love received within the infinite being of the source of all things. We are concerned here, in a true sense, with the logic of infinity, and the analogy has to be qualified precisely at the point where the spectre of tritheism looms. It is qualified right from the start by the recognition that we are dealing with the self-differentiation of the one infinite source of all, and further qualified by the doctrine of perichoresis, that doctrine of the mutual indwelling and interpenetration of the persons of the Trinity, which, however much it may puzzle the modern theologian, provided the modern poet, as we saw at the beginning, with the focus and the climax of his poem.

3

Jesus, God incarnate

The Christian doctrine of the Incarnation is one of the two central doctrines which set out the *unique* features of Christian faith in God. Christianity shares with many other religions belief in an infinite and transcendent God, the source of the world's being and of all its values. It recognises that in every part of the world traditions of religious belief and religious experience have made it possible for men and women to enjoy the blessedness of spiritual life and of the knowledge and love of God. But the Christian doctrine of the Incarnation expresses the conviction of Christians that this God has made himself known more fully, more specifically and more personally, by taking our human nature into himself, by coming amongst us as a particular man, without in any way ceasing to be the eternal and infinite God.

The other central doctrine is that of the Trinity. The reason why the doctrines of the Incarnation and Trinity go together is partly a matter of history and partly a matter of rational reflection. It was because the early Christians, in the light of the resurrection of Jesus from the dead, came to recognise his divinity and to experience him as the self-revelation of God that they perceived the necessity of believing that God himself, in his own being, exists in an internal relationship of love given and love received. That love, they saw, was mirrored in the relationship of Jesus to the Father. That same love they experienced in their own lives as poured out upon them and as a relationship in which they too were caught up and could come to share. But they also came to realise that the very notion of a God who is love requires us to think in terms of an internally differentiated and relational deity.

This may sound complicated, but the essence of the matter is quite simple. On the one hand we admit the greatness and transcendence of God. No religious mind can deny the ultimate mystery of God. The richness of his inner being far surpasses our power of comprehension. On the other hand we believe that this mysterious and ineffable God, out of pure love for mankind, has made himself known to us, in the most direct and comprehensible way possible, by coming amongst us as one of us, and sharing our life, its heights and depths, its joys and sorrows.

To believe in God incarnate, then, is to believe that God has chosen *this* way of making himself known and drawing us to himself. The doctrine involves taking very seriously both the divinity and the humanity of Jesus Christ. While it is primarily a doctrine about God, so that God himself, in one of the modes of his eternal being, is to be thought of as the subject of all the predicates we use in speaking of Jesus Christ, nevertheless the doctrine also asserts the real humanity of Jesus. In no way do we follow the 'docetic' tendencies of early Christianity, which found it hard to believe, for example, that Jesus shared the limitations of human psychology and cognition. This is to say that for Christian belief the Incarnation involved God's subjecting himself to the limitations of real humanity in order to achieve his purposes of revelation and reconciliation.

According to this doctrine of the Incarnation, the man Jesus cannot be thought of apart from his being God incarnate. Or rather, so to think of him is to abstract from the full reality of what was taking place at that time in history. Jesus was not just a particularly good man whom God decided to adopt. Rather the whole story of God's relation to the world is to be seen as pivoted around his personal presence and action here in our midst in Jesus Christ.

The moral and spiritual force of this doctrine is very great. In the first place we can see that God in Christ takes upon *himself* responsibility for all the world's ills. God bears the brunt of suffering and evil by subjecting *himself* to their cruelty and horror. By so doing, he reveals, as he could in no other way, the reality and depth and costly nature of his forgiving love. And by this identification of himself with us and our predicament he draws us to himself in an utterly moral and personal way.

For in the second place it is the personal presence of God this side of the divide between infinite and finite that is supremely revelatory to us of who God is. By this act, God overcomes the vagueness and the dread that limit the experience of God which elsewhere and otherwise men can and do enjoy. If Jesus is God *in person*, then our knowledge of God has an intelligible personal human focus. In Jesus' character and acts we see the character and acts of God himself in terms we can readily understand. At the same time God does not overwhelm us in his self-revelation. Instead he invites and wins our personal response.

This presence and action of God, here in our midst in person, cannot be thought of as a repeatable affair. If God is one, only one man can *be* God incarnate. Several people can manifest similar general characteristics and thus, perhaps, illustrate certain general truths about God's nature. But Jesus is *the* human face of God. The doctrine of the Incarnation is emptied of its point and value in referring to a real person-to-person encounter, if we suppose that a series of human beings from different times, places and cultures were all God incarnate. On such a view, God at once resumes the characteristics of vagueness and dread that the Christian doctrine of the Incarnation teaches us to overcome. Again, the unity of God and the uniqueness of the Incarnation lead Christianity to postulate and hope for the unification of humanity under God in Christ, whether here or in eternity.

The particularity of the Incarnation, the fact that if God was to come to us in person it would have to be at a particular time

23

and place in history, certainly, as I say, involves seeing the whole creation and the whole of human history as organised around or pivoted upon a brief slice of space–time in the history of the ancient Middle East. It also means that we in the twentieth century and all other human beings at other times and places, however long human history lasts, cannot enjoy precisely the same face-to-face human encounter with God incarnate that the disciples and other contemporaries of Jesus in Palestine enjoyed. Our personal commerce with God is through the spiritual and sacramental presence of the risen and ascended Christ. But the point remains that this is the spiritual and sacramental presence of the one who did tread the hills of Palestine, whose character and acts we read about in the Gospels. Again it needs to be stressed that the spiritual sense of the presence of God here and now requires that human focusing in the Jesus of Nazareth of nearly 2,000 years ago, if we are to enjoy the precision and clarity of God's self-disclosure through incarnation. Not that the humanity of God is a thing of the past only. The risen Christ's glorified humanity, we believe, is permanently taken into God, though it is not manifest to us at present – that is part of our future expectation. But for the present it is by his spiritual and sacramental presence that Jesus becomes *our* contemporary and reveals God to us here and now.

To suppose that God can and does relate himself to us and make himself known to us in this particular way, over and above the intimations of his reality and nature which religion in general provides, does, of course, imply that it is *possible* for him to do so. But who are we to say that the nature of God almighty, the infinite and eternal ground of our being, is such as to render this impossible? On the contrary, Christianity has taught us to see the power of God specifically made known in the weak human life of Jesus, his eternity in the temporal span of Jesus' life, his inner trinitarian relations in the prayers of Jesus to the Father and the gift of the Spirit to the Church.

We have no basis at all for saying that God *cannot* be such as to be able, without ceasing to be God, to unite his creation to himself first in an incarnate life, and then in and through our response to the risen and ascended one.

When we reflect on the historical evidence for these remarkable but central doctrines of Christianity, we need to beware of thinking that historical evidence alone must be seen to *necessitate* such an interpretation before we can allow ourselves to accept it. Of course the historical facts must be seen to *allow* or even to *suggest* this interpretation, if it is to be at all credible. We have to do justice to the impression made by Jesus, to the belief in his resurrection, and to the rapid growth of 'high' Christologies. But historical evidence alone cannot compel assent. We have also to reckon with Christian experience of the risen Christ down the ages, including that of our friends and of ourselves. And particularly, I think, we need to rediscover what I have called the moral and spiritual force of the doctrine of the Incarnation, the sense it makes of the relation between God and his creation, and the anticipations it yields, together with the doctrines of the Resurrection and Ascension, of the ultimate destiny of God's creation.

Current theological scepticism on these matters results from a narrowness of vision, an attempt to see the world as it is now construed in the natural and human sciences as being related tangentially to a mysterious, hidden and, one has to interpolate, extremely vague, divine ground or spirit. But the theologian must stick to his last. A theist is one who sees all creation, all religion and all history as the field of divine action and self-disclosure. Moreover he conceives of the whole story as moving in a particular direction to an ultimate goal or consummation. In the history of religions, several different ways of construing all this have emerged and been developed. In Christian theism, the central focus of the whole picture has been the life, death and resurrection of God incarnate, in which the infinite and eternal God has made himself both knowable and credible, and given us at once a present source of personal knowledge of himself, and an anticipation of the ultimate end, which we picture as a kingdom where Christ is king.

4

The moral and religious value of the Incarnation

An important factor in the assessment of our contemporary christological debates is the moral and religious value discernible in incarnational Christology. It is one factor only and cannot stand by itself. Only if the doctrine of the Incarnation is true may we commend it for its moral and religious value. We have no use for Plato's 'noble lie'. But the questions of truth and value are not entirely separate. While it would be improper to urge the value of the doctrine as the sole ground for thinking it true, it is not unreasonable to suppose that its perceived value may be an indication of its truth. In attempting to give a justification of the Chalcedonian formula, Austin Farrer observed: 'Look here: the longer I go on trying to tell you about this, the more I become convinced that the job that really wants doing is to expound the formula rather than to justify it; or, anyhow, that the justification required is identical with exposition.'[1] This may be going a bit far, but certainly part of the justification of the doctrine consists in exposition of its inner rationality, and that includes its moral and religious value. At the very least it may be said that insensitivity to the value of incarnational Christology can lead to a somewhat casual attitude to the historical, experiential and rational grounds for thinking the doctrine to be true.

It is no easy matter to assess the moral and religious value of different ways of understanding God and his relation to the world. This is a well-known problem in the comparative study of religion, although it is not our primary concern here. Our christological disputes are an internal matter of Christian self-understanding, and we do not have to cope directly with the problem of dialogue between radically different value systems. On the other hand, we are concerned with what have traditionally been taken to be the distinctive doctrines of Christianity, which mark it out from other world faiths. And it can be argued that our assessment of the respective strengths and weaknesses of incarnational and non-incarnational Christology within the sphere of Christian self-understanding is bound to be affected by our assessment of the moral and religious value of Christianity among the world religions. So it needs to be said that such comparison and dialogue, for all their difficulty, are not impossible. A simple example of such imagined dialogue is to be found in Ninian Smart's *A Dialogue of Religions*.[2]

I concentrate here, however, on the discussion internal to Christian self-understanding. I begin rather negatively with some comments on the moral and religious value of what has been said by recent critics of incarnational Christology. I then attempt to bring out, positively, the moral and religious value of the doctrine of the Incarnation, first in my own words, then with examples both from popular piety and contemporary theology. I conclude with some brief remarks about the implications of incarnational belief for Christian ethics.

Critics of incarnational Christology from within the Christian Church have no business to be telling us that the onus of proof lies with defenders of the tradition. Whether they like it or not, they live in and out of a tradition of faith, expressed in the creeds and confessions of the Church, which is undeviatingly trinitarian and incarnational in its understanding of God and of Christ. It is up to them to make out a case against incarnational and for non-incarnational Christology. Since our concern here is with the moral and religious nature of the Incarnation, I say nothing about the evidence for the doctrine and little about its logical coherence, except to show in passing that recent critics are much too ready to cry contradiction.

I begin by asking two related questions: have the critics shown a proper moral and religious sensitivity to what they are criticising? And does the *non*-incarnational Christology which they advocate possess the moral and religious value which they claim for *it*?

My first group of worries – about the seriousness with which the tradition is being taken by those who wish to question it – is liable to rebound upon my own arguments. For it is only too easy on both sides of this dispute to set up caricatures of opponents' views in order to have an easy target for demolition. Yet again I stress that the onus of proof lies with the attack, not with the defence, if it is Christian self-understanding that is in question. And one is bound to say that recent criticism of the doctrine of the Incarnation has shown quite astonishing moral and religious insensitivity to what is under discussion. What is one to make, for instance, of Goulder's reference to 'a landing-take-off-and-landing myth.'[3] in respect of the Christologies of Paul and John? It is interesting to compare Goulder's treatment of these matters with that of Bultmann. I do not know if there is more or less to be said for Goulder's hypothesis of a Samaritan origin for Christian incarnational doctrine than for Bultmann's hypothesis of a gnostic redeemer myth (I dare say there is not much to be said for either), but at least Bultmann showed, in his commentary on the Fourth Gospel, a fine sensitivity to the moral and religious value of what came to expression there.

Another example, this time of sheer perversity in moral judgement, is to be found in Cupitt's essay in *The Myth of God Incarnate*. The burden of his argument is that the Christian doctrine of the Incarnation has reinforced the conception of religion as monarchical and authoritarian. 'As the manifest Absolute in history', he writes, 'Christ became the basis of the Christian empire and of political and ecclesiastical power in the present age.' 'Inevitably', he goes on, 'Christianity became, or rather was deliberately made absolutist and authoritarian.'[4] It is in the claim that this development was inevitable and that these tendencies have an essential connection with the doctrine of the Incarnation that the perversity of Cupitt's judgement lies. For it is quite clear from the New Testament and from Christian piety down the ages that what has given Christianity its characteristic moral and religious force is the conviction that its Lord had humbled himself and taken the form of a servant.

A third example – and here we touch on the question of coherence – can be found in the cavalier treatment which both Hick and Cupitt give to kenotic Christology, especially in respect of its insistence on the human limitations of Jesus' self-knowledge. Kenotic Christology, although its early versions in German and English theology were justly criticised for metaphysical naivety, has in fact been refined and expounded with great care and penetration in the writing of theologians such as Frank Weston, O. C. Quick and Austin Farrer. In particular, the moral force of the doctrine that God, in becoming man, subjects himself to the conditions of human knowledge and self-knowledge, so that, *qua* human subject, he experiences his identity with God in terms solely of his relation to his heavenly Father (that relation being seen by us as reflecting in God–man terms the inner God–God relations of the Blessed Trinity) – the moral force of this doctrine is very great. God is seen here to have humbled himself in order to make himself known and knowable as the one who, out of pure love, comes to us as a servant and loves his own 'unto the end'.[5] Kenotic Christology enables us to see that, by incarnation, the humanity of God is that of a particular human being, a first-century Jewish man. As Austin

Farrer put it: 'God the Son on earth is a fullness of holy life within the limit of mortality.' But Hick, in his preface to the paperback edition of *God and the Universe of Faiths*, refers dismissively to the 'new paradox of God incarnate who does not know that he is God incarnate'.[6] To refer dismissively to the notion that Jesus was God but was unaware of it is to fail to grasp the point of kenotic Christology. It is to assume that there is no alternative between a thoroughly docetic Christ and a purely human Jesus. But in fact the tradition has carefully distinguished what can be said of the human subject, Jesus, from what can be said of the divine subject, God the Son, whose human expression and vehicle, in his incarnate life, the human subject, Jesus, is. (As such, of course, it is, uniquely, not an independent human subject – hence the doctrine of 'anhypostasia'.) Clearly, God, *qua* God, is aware of who he is and what he is doing, but, *qua* man (i.e. as Jesus), his self-awareness is limited to a filial sense of dependence on the Father. For this reason incarnational Christology attributes two consciousnesses, not to Jesus, but to God incarnate. This distinction has been carefully mapped by Geach, in his treatment of the logic of what has been called 'reduplicative propositions'.[7] It emerges that much depends on what one sees as the primary subject of christological statements. It is no good suggesting that *Jesus*, *qua* God, would do this, and, *qua* man, would do that. That would already be to confuse the natures by predicating unlimited divinity of the man instead of predicating real humanity of God incarnate. The primary subject of all christological statements is God. It is God, *qua* God, who cannot die, and it is God incarnate, i.e. God, *qua* man, who suffers and dies for our salvation. Nor is there any question of sundering the natures here, when it is made quite clear that we are not talking of two separate individuals, but of the divine substance, which is such as to include within its own subjectivity the human subject, Jesus, as the expression and vehicle of God's incarnate life.

It is noteworthy that accusations of incoherence at this point depend upon construing the divine nature anthropomorphically. Of course one *man* cannot be identified with another or express himself through another. But the infinite trinitarian God, we are invited to suppose, can, without ceasing to be God, in one of the modes of his eternal being, live out a human life and suffer a human fate. Of course we cannot picture this to ourselves, but anything we could picture would not be God. Far from incarnational Christology involving anthropomorphism, to suppose that God, without ceasing to be God, anthropomorphises himself, is to operate with an utterly unanthropomorphic notion of God.

Although I regard insensitivity to the scope of classical Christian theism and to the elements of kenoticism which it has shown itself to be capable of embracing as being primarily a theoretical theological fault, I stress here that it has the consequence of rendering these writers incapable of appreciating the value of the incarnation.

When we turn to the question of the moral and religious value of the non-incarnational Christologies offered in its place, one is bound to say that they look pretty vague and thin. It is very difficult to see why we, in the twentieth century, should take the purely human Jesus to be 'the man of universal destiny' (Goulder). The human parallels which Goulder offers have the effect of demoting Jesus to the status of one exemplar of selfless love among others. But the community of love which came into being as a result of the events concerning Jesus is sustained down the centuries by more than the example of his martyrdom.

Cupitt's Jesus is a more austere and less intelligible figure. We are to recapture, it seems, something of his sense of the immediacy of God, and of his eschatological faith. But who can say what this really means? Cupitt writes: 'The most religiously-substantial thing we can reasonably confidently associate with Jesus is his voice, his peculiar form of saving

32

linguistic action.'[8] But what is this, compared with the spiritual and sacramental presence of the risen and ascended Christ?

Houlden speaks of 'the centrality of Jesus for all that concerns man's understanding of God' and indeed of God's 'deep and intimate involvement'[9] with the world. But what do these words mean when the beliefs that give them some concrete basis are jettisoned in favour of 'experience'?

I have similar difficulties with Hick's suggestion that God's patient love is revealed in the world by the death of martyrs.[10] How, one may ask, does someone else's death reveal *God*'s love? And when Frances Young writes, very movingly, that the Cross of Jesus constitutes 'above all, a revelation of divine involvement in the suffering and evil of the world',[11] it seems that she is trying to retain the moral and religious value of the traditional doctrine in a context that cannot bear that weight. As Michael Ramsey pointed out, in comment on a radio discussion of these issues, the religious value of the Cross for us – in face of suffering and evil in our own lives – consists in our being able to see God there in person (not just by sympathy with someone else).

The sharp polarity between what, following O. C. Quick, one may call the modernist and the liberal elements in current non-incarnational Christology is brought out by a consideration of the respective positions of Nineham in *The Myth* and Lampe in the Bampton Lectures. For Nineham, a combination of historical scepticism and historical relativism makes it impossible to accord to Jesus himself the moral and religious significance that even the other authors of *The Myth* wish still to find in him. Nineham, by contrast, finds the value of Christianity to reside in the full and rich relationship to God[12] which life in the Church makes possible for us today. But how can this be, when both the historical basis and the doctrinal shape of the Church's tradition have been overthrown? At the other pole, Lampe still wishes to speak of Jesus' 'perfect and unbroken response to the Father'[13] as of supreme exemplary significance for his followers ever since. But how, in non-incarnational terms, can one account for such unique perfection at one point in past history, let alone for its continuing import across the centuries? On either view, the supposition that the Church, the supposed bearer of moral and religious value down the ages, has radically misconstrued the nature and place of Christ in respect of our knowledge of God casts grave doubt on the viability of the doctrine of providence involved (a Church-centred providence in Nineham's case, a Jesus-centred providence in Lampe's).

In his introductory essay to *The Myth*, Wiles very properly asks how much of the Christian religion would survive the abandonment of incarnational belief in its strong metaphysical sense. That book's own instances of non-incarnational Christology suggest that very little that is distinctive does survive, and that what does so survives only by relying on elements in the tradition which presuppose a fuller incarnational understanding.

I am not arguing that there is absolutely nothing of moral or religious worth in the writings under consideration. We find in them much that expresses a pure faith in God, a maturity of spiritual perception (I think here particularly of Lampe's Bampton Lectures), and a conviction of the authenticity and value of religious experience as such. Such elements these Christian writers share with men of all pure ethical monotheistic faiths. But Christianity has claimed to introduce something further, something new and unique into the history of religions. And it is the moral and religious value of this 'something more' that has been lost in non-incarnational Christology.

What, then, is the moral and religious value of the Incarnation? I shall first summarise this under four headings: (1) revelation and personal knowledge of God; (2) trinitarian belief; (3) the problem of evil and the atonement; (4) presence and participation.

(1) In the first place, the moral and religious value of the Incarnation lies in the greatly increased potential for human knowledge of God and personal union with God introduced by God's own presence and acts, in human form, this side of the gap between Creator and creature. The character of Christ *is* for us the revealed character of God, and becomes the criterion for our understanding of the nature and will of God. In a sense the humanity of Christ mediates God to us, but in another sense God's love is communicated to us immediately by God's own incarnate presence here in our midst. It is perfectly true that we today are not face to face with God incarnate as the disciples were. But the inevitable limitations of that particularity are overcome, as I shall stress below, by his spiritual and sacramental presence and activity, by means of which God's personal self-revelation in Jesus is universalised. My point here is that the story of Jesus gives that universal activity of God its concrete, particular and utterly personal form.

The humanity of Christ is, of course, for Christian understanding, permanently taken into God. The risen Christ remains the focus and channel of our knowledge of God and the key by which all other experience of God is converted into personal knowledge of the Blessed Trinity.

(2) The trinitarian implications of Christology must be stressed further here, if we are to avoid an excessively individualised Jesus cult. Jesus reveals God to us, not only by his character and acts and passion, but also by his prayers to the Father, by his resurrection, and by the outpouring of the Spirit. But the doctrine of the Trinity has an independent place, as well, in our assessment of the moral and religious value of incarnational Christology. For in forcing us to think of God in richer, relational terms, as the fullness of love given and love received within his own being prior to creation, it

resolves that impasse in pure monotheism which results from
conceiving of God on the analogy of an isolated individual.
Lampe claims that there is no need to project relationship into
God, since God participates immanently in his creatures'
reciprocities.[14] But this makes creation necessary to God, if
God is to enjoy the fullness of being as love. This, I submit,
is to introduce real incoherence into any religiously and
metaphysically satisfying concept of God.

(3) Thirdly, the moral and religious value of the Incarnation is seen in the way it confronts the world's evil. In happier
days, this point was seen by Hick, when he wrote:

> It is part of the meaning of christian monotheism that there is an
> ultimately responsible moral being, who is absolute goodness and
> love, whom we may trust amid the uncertainties and anxieties of the
> gradual unfolding of reality to us in time. We are led to this trust
> by seeing the divine responsibility at work on earth in the life of
> Christ. For there we see the Love which has ordained the long costly
> soul-making process entering into it and sharing with us in its
> inevitable pains and suffering.[15]

As was pointed out above in respect of Frances Young's
reference to the Cross of Christ, the moral force of this
depends on Christ's *being* God. One cannot accept responsibility for the world's ills through someone else. Hick now
wishes to stress God's 'participation in every pain'. But the
manner of this participation makes all the difference. Only if
we can say that God has *himself*, on the Cross, 'borne our sorrows' can we find him universally present 'in' the sufferings
of others. It is not a question of 'awareness' and 'sympathy'.
It is, as Whitehead put it, a matter of the 'fellow-sufferer who
understands'. This whole dimension of the Christian doctrine
of the Incarnation, its recognition of the costly nature of
God's forgiving love, and its perception that only a suffering
God is morally credible, is lost if God's involvement is
reduced to a matter of 'awareness' and 'sympathy'.

I come, thus somewhat indirectly, to the doctrine of the

Atonement, which, of course, has traditionally been held to spell out the chief moral and religious value of the Incarnation. As J. K. Mozely emphasised in his excellent essay in *Mysterium Christi* on 'Christology and Soteriology',[16] it is soteriological considerations that require us to think of Jesus as coming to the world from the side of God, and not as the highest stage in religious evolution. And certainly it is only if we can think of Jesus as being divine as well as being human that we can speak of his life and death and resurrection as of universal salvific significance for all men. The objectivity of the atonement consists in its being God's act for all. Unfortunately the manner in which this is so has been spelled out in a variety of theories of the atonement which are themselves open to grave moral objection, and this has led to revulsion from objective theories of the atonement and a failure to perceive the real moral significance of the Incarnation. Consequently it needs to be stated quite categorically that God's forgiving love does not depend on the death of Christ, but rather is manifested and enacted in it. It is precisely because the Spirit who converts our hearts and builds up our life in the Spirit is the Spirit of the crucified God that God's forgiveness and our reconciliation have the profoundly moral quality that has been the real inspiration of Christian piety down the ages, despite its often crude forms of expression. The costly and deeply moral nature of God's reconciling work was summarised by Austin Farrer thus: 'What, then, did God do for his people's redemption? He came amongst them, bringing his kingdom, and he let events take their human course. He set the divine life in human neighbourhood. Men discovered it in struggling with it and were captured by it crucifying it'.[17]

(4) Fourthly, the religious value of the Incarnation is seen in the christological and trinitarian concentration, in terms of which present Christian experience, worship and life are to be understood. As Moule has repeatedly stressed, it is conviction

of Christ as a living presence, both spiritually and sacramentally, that differentiates specifically Christian awareness of God from all other. Moreover Christian worship has never been conceived solely as a matter of response, in gratitude and adoration, by creatures to their Creator. It is rather a matter of being caught up into Christ's eternal offering to the Father, and of being indwelt by the Spirit, who, from within, draws us in worship into the inner life of God. Similarly, in the body of Christ, we become, by adoption and grace, instruments in the history of divine action, which is not only a matter of God's movement out towards his creation, but a movement back from creation to God. The specifically Christian insight is that this too, the movement from creation to God, takes place in God, through the humanity of Christ, and derivatively through ourselves, as we are united with Christ, alike in worship and work.

Before illustrating these central features of specifically Christian self-understanding from the writings of some contemporary theologians, I should like to indicate the way in which they come to simple, yet profound expression in Christian hymnody.

Fortunately the popular Christmas carols will ensure that Chalcedonian orthodoxy will be remembered long after *The Myth* is forgotten.

> Hark, hark! the wise eternal Word
> Like a weak infant cries;
> In form of servant is the Lord,
> And God in cradle lies.

The Passiontide hymns bring out the saving significance of the Incarnation:

> My song is love unknown
> My Saviour's love to me
> Love to the loveless shown,
> That they might lovely be.
> O who am I

> That for my sake
> My Lord should take
> Frail flesh and die?

St Patrick's Breastplate and the hymns of Cardinal Newman ensure that trinitarian faith finds expression in Christian worship, and I cannot resist quoting the second verse of F. W. Faber's little-sung hymn, 'Most ancient of all mysteries':

> When heaven and earth were yet unmade
> When time was yet unknown
> Thou in thy bliss and majesty
> Didst live and love alone.

The Eucharistic hymns preserve, most eloquently, that sense of the presence of the risen Christ by his Spirit which is the essence of living Christian faith:

> Thee we adore, O hidden Saviour, thee,
> Who in thy Sacrament art pleased to be;
> Both flesh and spirit in thy presence fail,
> Yet here thy Presence we devoutly hail.

> And now, O Father, mindful of the love
> That bought us, once for all, on Calvary's Tree
> And having with us him that pleads above
> We here present, we here spread forth to thee
> That only Offering perfect in thine eyes,
> The one true, pure, immortal Sacrifice.

It is of no avail to say that these hymns still have the power to move as myth; for their moving power consists in the real content of these words, and if all attempts to articulate the doctrinal content of such poetic forms of expression are to be dismissed as incoherent, then the power to move is lost. We are not moved by nonsense.

The moral and religious value of the doctrines of the Incarnation and the Trinity comes to more sophisticated expression in much contemporary theology, both Catholic

39

and Protestant. I select four books to illustrate this: Hans Urs von Balthasar's *Love Alone: The Way of Revelation*, T. F. Torrance's *God and Rationality*, Jürgen Moltmann's *The Crucified God*, and Eberhard Jüngel's *God as the Mystery of the World.*

Von Balthasar's little book presents, in summary form, the main thesis of his so-called 'theological aesthetic', that men are won over into loving contemplation of the trinitarian God by the revealed glory of God's own act of love in incarnation and the Cross. Scripture and doctrine alike are only witnesses to 'the concrete, incarnate God, who interprets himself as the absolute love of God'. Liberal Protestant theology, says von Balthasar, makes 'the revelation of the Cross and Resurrection innocuous by transforming it into a banal ''teaching'' or parable – instead of accepting the form itself realistically as the dramatic appearance of God's trinitarian love and as the Trinity's loving struggle for mankind'.[18] Earlier, he has pointed out the way in which God's act of love in incarnation reveals the Trinity.

The obedient love of the Son for the Father is certainly the model for human love before the majesty of God but more than that, it is the supreme image of divine love itself appearing. For it is precisely in the Kenosis of Christ (and nowhere else) that the *inner* majesty of God's love appears, of God who 'is love' (1 John 4.8) and therefore trinity.[19]

He has already emphasised that where 'Christ is referred to as ''the image of God'', the words are not to be taken as a mythical statement because the world of myth has been for ever left behind since the Incarnation'.[20] Von Balthasar's insistence on the enacted and revealed love of God himself as constituting the source and ground of our response in love and contemplation brings out very clearly the fact that, in this paper, we are talking about the religious value of the Incarnation, and only derivatively of the religious value of the *doctrine* of the Incarnation.

T. F. Torrance addresses himself to the articulation of a

specifically Christian understanding of the relation between
God and man with great theological penetration. In a lecture,
entitled 'The Word of God and the Response of Man', in his
God and Rationality, he speaks of the 'Word' of God as that 'mode
of His Being in which God goes forth to meet man, freely
relating His divine Life to him within the conditions of his
creaturely nature, and in which He sustains man in his meeting
with God, enabling him freely to relate his human life to the
majesty of the divine Nature'.[21] At this point I would stress
the latter aspect of the doctrine; for it is the Incarnation which
not only brings God to us, but creates the conditions in which
our own response to Him can be made. God not only enters
our estranged existence 'in order to struggle with the perverse
nature of an alienated creation, to meet the full hostility of evil
by accepting and bearing it in Himself', God incarnate also
himself constitutes the perfect *human* response, by incorporation into which we are enabled to respond. It is this element
which is so notably absent in liberal Protestant theology, namely
the fact that man's response to God takes place in God – in
the Spirit, through incorporation into the Body of Christ.

My third example of contemporary theology in which the
moral and religious value of the Incarnation is seen is Jürgen
Moltmann's *The Crucified God*. There is much in that book with
which we might well wish to quarrel, but the central chapter,
which has the book's own title, constitutes a remarkable attempt to think through what it means for our concept of God to
say that Christ's Cross is God's Cross in our world. 'With the
Christian message of the cross of Christ', he writes,

something new and strange has come into the metaphysical world.
For this faith must understand the deity of God from the event of the
suffering and death of the Son of God and thus bring about a fundamental change in the orders of being of metaphysical thought and
the value tables of religious feeling. It must think of the suffering of
Christ as the power of God and the death of Christ as God's
potentiality.[22]

41

An indication of the way in which this is spelled out in terms of its moral and religious value is given in the following quotation:

If Christian belief thinks in trinitarian terms, it says that forsaken men are already taken up by Christ's forsakenness into the divine history and that we 'live in God', because we participate in the eschatological life of God by virtue of the death of Christ. God is, God is in us, God suffers in us, where love suffers. We participate in the trinitarian process of God's history.[23]

I quote this passage because it points up the folly of suggesting that the suffering of God with all suffering creatures can be affirmed without a doctrine of the Incarnation or, even more implausibly, that to affirm God's unique personal presence in the Cross of Christ is to make God somehow less present to the whole of suffering humanity. On the contrary, God's presence with suffering humanity can only be affirmed on the basis of God's own suffering in the Cross of Christ.

My last example of creative incarnational and trinitarian theology is Eberhard Jüngel's *God as the Mystery of the World*. This important book suggests some modification of the trinitarian doctrine so far adumbrated in this paper. While Jüngel makes it absolutely clear that to say that 'God is love' is to posit an internally differentiated, relational deity, he also suggests that the self-sacrificial nature of the divine love is only seen in the love of God for the world, a love that meant for God himself not only the *sending* of the Son, but his passion and death.[24] This is very different from saying that God needs the world in order to love. It is rather to insist that God's inner nature as lover and beloved is enacted and manifested in Creation and the Cross.

In mentioning these four books, I can do little more than hint at the possibilities in theological exploration of the moral and religious value of the Incarnation. But a factor of considerable importance for our present debate emerges from a study of these writings. It is clear that these authors stand firmly within the tradition of incarnational and trinitarian orthodoxy, and yet break with at least the most powerful strand in the tradition over both the impassibility of God and the degree to which an element of kenoticism is to be welcomed and embraced within a broadly orthodox position. It is, of course, a matter of judgement whether these developments (both, it should be stressed of great moral and religious significance) constitute a break with the tradition of comparable dimensions to that proposed in non-incarnational Christology. I am bound to say that to my mind there is no comparison. The developments regarding our understanding of the suffering of God and of the human limitations of Jesus' self-consciousness are quite legitimate developments within incarnational and trinitarian theology, while the rejection of the doctrines of the Incarnation and the Trinity marks a decisive break with the faith of the Christian Church.

The appeal to the over-arching authority of the incarnational and trinitarian tradition is not, it should be emphasised, a bare appeal to authority. The authority of the tradition lies fairly and squarely in its content, in the way it commends itself to historical judgement, to rational comprehension and to experiential authentication. In particular, as has been urged in this chapter, its authority lies in the moral and religious value to be found in it.

I append a note on the implications of incarnational belief for Christian ethics. It has often been pointed out that a number of ethical consequences follow from belief that God's love is enacted and made manifest in the Incarnation and the Cross. In the first place it is suggested that this shows that the material is not alien to the spiritual, but that the body is to be seen as the vehicle of the spirit. This is spelled out further in Christian sacramental theology, and often generalised into a sacramental view of the universe. In the second place, the Incarnation has been taken as the pattern of Christian

43

ministry, as a matter of involvement and service in every area of human life. This includes what may be singled out as a third implication, namely, involvement in the communal and political structures of human life. On this basis, political theology is a valid deduction from the Gospel of the Incarnation. If it is argued that the recorded teaching of Jesus hardly bears this out, the reply must be given that Christian social ethics are based on principles drawn from the whole event and action of the Incarnation.

No doubt I shall be told that these general principles of sacramental life, involved service, and political commitment do not depend on the truth of incarnational Christology, but can be argued for and commended irrespective of Christian doctrine. No doubt they can. That is why the bulk of this chapter was argued on other grounds. But the question remains an open one, whether other systems of religious or indeed non-religious belief have in fact fostered and have in fact had it in them to sustain such incarnational practice.

5

Further remarks on the 'Myth' debate

THE LOGICAL COHERENCE OF THE DOCTRINE OF THE INCARNATION

It is certainly difficult, indeed paradoxical, to suppose that a human life lived out within the framework of first-century Jewish consciousness could actually *be* the incarnate life of God himself in one of the modes of his infinite and eternal being. But this doctrine is not overthrown by setting out travestied versions of it, nor is it overthrown by pressing the details of all-too-human analogies. It is a travesty to suggest that, for kenotic Christology, divinity is predicated of Jesus' humanity. That is certainly to confuse the natures. We predicate divinity of Jesus, because we believe his humanity to be the vehicle and expression of the eternal Son. There is no conversion of the Godhead into flesh. To think that is to operate with some crude picture of two kinds of stuff. Nor is there any reason to postulate three consciousnesses where God incarnate is concerned. All we need is Jesus' own sense of filial dependence on the one hand, and God's awareness of his (God's) own acts through incarnation on the other.

In his reply,[1] Cupitt attacks my metaphor of 'inclusion' – the suggestion that Jesus' human self-consciousness is 'included' within the divine self-consciousness as its vehicle and expression. Cupitt asks how we are to imagine it, as though our talk of God is decided by what we can imagine! He goes on not only anthropomorphically but Cupittomorphically by talking of some hypothetical division of his own personality, as though that were a basis for advance in theological understanding. His objection, generalised, turns out to rest on the highly anthropomorphic picture of two human individuals and the impossibility of our thinking of them as identical. But that is no way to explore the logic of God-talk.

A similar fault appears in Goulder's more careful statement of the objection from alleged incoherence.[2] He tells us a story about the Vice-Chancellor, changed utterly, so that there is no continuity by which identity-talk could be justified. But this all-too-human analogy does not begin to meet the case. We are not suggesting that God becomes an utterly changed God, or that Jesus becomes a different man from the man he was before. The continuity in incarnation is quite clear. It is the continuity of God's own act in incarnation, manifesting, in another mode, his steadfast love and limitless grace.

These objections fail because they themselves depend wholly on what we can imagine anthropomorphically. I notice that accusations of anthropomorphism come from critics who themselves, at least in considering their opponents' views, think only anthropomorphically. There is a sense, of course, in which, for the classical Christian tradition, it is true that God anthropomorphises himself in coming amongst us as one of us, but that can only be said when we are operating with a totally unanthropomorphic concept of God, when we train ourselves to think not in images, but theologically of the eternal and infinite God, who is such as to be able to live out a truly human life on earth for our sake, and to relate himself to himself in an earthly parable of the Blessed Trinity.

I said that the doctrine of the Incarnation was paradoxical, and so it should be, if human words are to be used to precipitate our minds beyond the natural into thought of the transcendent. This is the function of paradox in religious language, as Ian Ramsey was always keen to show.[3] It is not a matter of rejoicing in straight contradiction at the single mundane level of talk about two human individuals. The paradoxes are a sign that we have to stop thinking anthropomorphically; and they are a tool for thinking theologically about the one who cannot be 'comprehended' with clear-cut univocal terms. We have to learn how to use these tools. It is certainly not the case that 'anything goes' when we begin, as Ramsey encouraged us to do, to explore the logic of irreducible religious paradox. I offer my remarks on kenotic Christology as an example of the kind of discrimination that one can at least try to make in this area.

THE INCARNATION AND MODERN THEOLOGY

In each generation, theologians have to explore and restate the doctrines of the Church in the light of advancing knowledge, both of science and of history. Thus the doctrine of Creation has been restated in the light of our vastly increased understanding of cosmology and evolution. But it remains the doctrine of Creation. We affirm, with the tradition, that this whole evolving universe depends for its being and purpose on the creative will and act of God. The doctrine of the Fall has also been restated, perhaps even more radically, in the light of this same knowledge and of the history of man. But it remains the doctrine of the Fall. We affirm, with the tradition, that man, through the pressures both of heredity and environment and through the corruption of his will, falls very far short of the divine intention, and stands in need of redemption. The doctrine of the Incarnation, too, has been restated in the light of greatly increased historical, cultural and psychological realism about what it is to be a man, and a man of first-century Palestine at that. But it remains the doctrine of the Incarnation. We affirm, with the tradition, that, out of his great love, and in order to reconcile men to himself, God, without ceasing to be God, came amongst us

47

as one of us, making himself vulnerable to suffering and
evil.

In each case, such restatement is a matter of advance rather
than retreat. Theologically speaking, the doctrine of Creation
is more profoundly grasped when it is articulated in terms of
metaphysical dependence; the doctrine of the Fall is more
profoundly grasped when it is articulated in terms of the
radical gap between human achievement and the divine purpose; and the doctrine of the Incarnation is more profoundly
grasped when it is articulated in terms of kenosis – when the
human vehicle or expression of God's presence and action in
our midst is taken absolutely seriously in every facet of his
human being.

There is surely a sense in which we may speak of a 'literal'
incarnation. Literal uses of words are to be contrasted with
metaphorical uses. One of the dictionary definitions of
'literal' says that it is applied 'to the relatively primary sense
of a word'. Clearly many words used of God are used in
secondary senses, metaphorically, that is – as when we call
God 'the Rock of Ages'. With other words, the case is not
so clear. Aquinas distinguished the analogical from the
metaphorical on the grounds that some perfections, such as
love, mind and will, are predicated of God as, in reality, their
primary exemplar, on which their normal everyday exempli-
fications ultimately depend.[4] This complicates the issue,
since there is still a sense (Aquinas calls it the 'modus
significandi') in which the ordinary uses are primary and the
theological uses secondary and extended. But in the order of
being (the 'res significata') the priority is reversed. This
means that, by contrast with metaphorical talk, analogical
talk ceases to be figurative and secondary. One might say that
the analogical sense comes to constitute the primary 'literal'
sense for fundamental theology. Fortunately these complica-
tions need not bother us here; for there is a third class of
words used in religion and theology in neither metaphorical

nor analogical senses. These are words like 'holy', 'sin', and in-deed 'God', which are coined for religious purposes in the first place. Their religious or theological use is in every way primary. There can be no question but that they are used 'liter-ally' in such contexts. 'Incarnation' falls into this category. The dictionary tells us that its earliest and still prevalent sense is that of the incarnation of God in Christ. It is general uses, meaning 'embodiment', as when we say that 'the Senior Tutor is the veritable incarnation of good sense', that are the secondary, metaphorical senses. We can indeed speak of a 'literal' incarnation.

Of course the fact that a word like 'incarnation' is used in its primary sense for a mysterious and baffling act of the transcendent God in making himself personally present and known in human form means that it is by no means a clear-cut, easily comprehensible and fully articulated concept. We do not grasp the essence of the Incarnation any more than we grasp the essence of God. But the literal uses of all these special religious words inevitably include mystery. They are specifically designed to refer, literally, to that which necessa-rily eludes our full cognitive grasp.

I might add that I have no hesitation whatsoever in stan-ding by what I wrote in my *Theology* article:[5] 'The human life lived and the death died have been held quite literally to be the human life and death of God himself in one of the modes of his own eternal being' – though I grant that that takes us back to the *analogy* of *being* ('analogy', as I said, being included within the 'literal', by contrast with the 'meta-phorical').

THE UNIQUENESS OF THE INCARNATION

From time to time the suggestion is made that there is no reason why, if incarnation is possible at all, it should have taken place only once rather than at many points in the history of religions.

This opens up the whole question of the relation between Christianity and the other world faiths.

The suggestion that Jesus might have been one of many incarnations of God in human history betrays a complete failure to appreciate what the doctrine of the Incarnation, in classical Christian faith, has been held to state. If God himself, in one of the modes of his being, has come into our world in person, to make himself personally known and to make himself vulnerable to the world's evil, in order to win our love and bind us to himself, we cannot suppose that he might have done so more than once. For only one man can actually *be* God to us, if God himself is one. We are to posit relation in God, but not a split personality. Only one actual human person can be the vehicle and expression of the one God on earth. To think of many human beings as incarnations of God is to think of incarnation in a different sense – a derived metaphorical sense, namely, the embodiment of general characteristics. It is true that a whole number of loving, self-sacrificial men and women can manifest something of the loving-kindness of God in their lives. But that doesn't make them God himself in person.

The scandal of particularity is only a scandal to those who have failed to appreciate what God has done. Indeed it is the particularity of God's action in 'setting his love in human neighbourhood' (Farrer) that makes God credible and lovable in an utterly personal way. The nub of the matter is what we mean by personal knowledge. I can know many facts about another at second hand from many sources. But when I meet that other face to face, I begin to to know him personally – a totally different existential relation from what was the case before. Admittedly that is not a fair analogy for the relation between Christianity and other religions; for God is present to all men in hidden ways, by his Spirit. He is not just the unknown transcendent God. He is immanent in the whole world, particularly in the worlds of religion and ethics. But here we have to spell out the difference between immanence and incarnation. Religious and moral experience can undoubtedly mediate God to us. We can enlarge on the opening verses of the letter to the Hebrews: God has not only spoken to us of old by the prophets, he has also spoken to us through mystical experience, ethical concern and human love; but he has now spoken to us by a Son. And the Son, we discover, is very God of very God, God's human face, reflecting God's own glory, and bearing the stamp of his nature.

This unique incarnation, in which all knowledge of God is taken up and transformed into personal encounter, is not an isolated bolt from the blue. For Christian understanding, the whole of history pivots on the event of Christ's coming. The wider context of the history of religion and ethics, and the narrower context of the history of Israel, are to be regarded as providentially ordered, preparing the way for the Incarnation. Moreover the whole future of man's relation to God, subsequent to the Incarnation, is channelled through Christ, risen and ascended. His glorified humanity remains the focus of our knowledge of God both now and in the eschaton.

Admittedly we have to go on to speak of Christ in universal terms. He is no longer to be thought of as restricted to the particular slice of space-time that we read about in the Gospels. Just as the men of the New Testament came very rapidly to think of him in cosmic terms as the one through whom the world was made and as the universal Logos of God, enlightening every man that comes into the world, so we look for his hidden, all-embracing presence in religion and ethics everywhere. But the specific, particular Incarnation remains the key, the clue, and the criterion both of God's way with man, and for man's future in God. That clue is ironed out, that focus blurred, if we take the Incarnation out of its total, world-historical context, and read it as one point among others of divine–human encounter. Christianity just is not like that. For better or for worse, the Incarnation provides a

51

total interpretative key by which all other knowledge of God is to be finally illuminated and transformed, just because it is God's own particular act in time and for eternity.

Consequently, I can make nothing of Wiles' objection[6] that if incarnation is possible, it ought to be achieved in all men. The Incarnation concerns God's dealings with us, now and for all time. He identifies himself with our lot in the closest possible way in order to draw us to him. I have argued that it makes no sense to suppose that he who made himself one of us might have been many of us. Still less sense (if that is possible) does it make to say that he might have been all of us. The purpose of the Incarnation was to establish a new relation between ourselves and God. But the Incarnation is not itself a *relation* between God and man. It includes that, admittedly, and Jesus' relation to the Father is the model for all divine–human relations. But the main point of the Incarnation is not a matter of relation at all. It is a matter of identity. Jesus *is* God incarnate – for our sake and our salvation. God draws near to us in Jesus. He is himself present and active precisely there. But he does not become you and me. To suggest that he might is not only a nonsense in itself. It makes nonsense of the purpose of the Incarnation, namely, the restoration of *relationship* between God and ourselves.

6

The propriety of the doctrine of the Incarnation as a way of interpreting Christ

For the larger part of their history, the Christian Churches have taught the doctrines of the Incarnation and the Trinity as central and essential to their faith. Their creeds, Councils and confessions, whatever their differences and whatever range of different interpretations they have permitted, have agreed in affirming that the central figure of the Gospels is to be understood not only as the revealer of God, but as himself the content of that revelation, God the Son made man for our salvation, and that the doctrine of God implied by that revelation is to be expressed in trinitarian terms. These are still, to a very large extent, the characteristic and peculiar beliefs of Christianity, in its Eastern Orthodox, Roman Catholic and Protestant forms. Nevertheless, since the Enlightenment and the rise of modern critical approaches both to scripture and to tradition, the propriety of these doctrines has been questioned. This questioning has been overwhelmingly a Protestant phenomenon, though there have been and are some indications of similar questioning in Roman Catholic theology at the turn of the century and today. Disregarding external critics of Christianity, we can point within the Christian Churches themselves to rationalist versions of the faith in which the eternal truths of reason (metaphysical and moral) have been held to constitute the essence of Christianity, deistic versions, which have sought to eliminate the notions of special revelation and divine action in the world, idealist versions, in which the concept of incarnation has been held to symbolise some universal identity of God and man, liberal Protestant versions, which have singled out either the God-consciousness of Jesus or his teaching as the crucial element in Christianity, and modernist versions, in which the life of the Church itself has been embraced as experientially self-authenticating, irrespective of its origins.

As this list implies, the word 'incarnation' can be borrowed in order to express some of these post-Enlightenment versions of the Christian faith; but it needs to be stressed at once that the sense of 'incarnation' whose propriety we are concerned with here is the classical sense, however varied its formulation, of God's self-revelation here on earth, not only in but as the man Jesus of Nazareth. We are concerned with ἐνανθρώπησις, to use the Greek term, with 'die Menschwerdung Gottes', an expression for which we sadly lack an exact equivalent in English. It is true that the Patristic Greek Lexicon lists three Nestorian or adoptionist uses of ἐνανθρώπησις, and it is true that the term 'Menschwerdung' can be given a universal Hegelian sense, but for the most part these Greek and German words enable us to focus our attention more precisely on the classical sense of 'the Incarnation' in which Christology is held to be concerned with the unique and unrepeatable act of God, in one of the modes of his being, in coming amongst us, living a human life and dying a human death. We are concerned, in other words, with the propriety of talk of Christ as 'vere Deus et vere homo', with the two natures doctrine, if you like, though we shall see some reason to doubt the propriety of the term 'nature'. On this view, the *doctrine* of the Incarnation is not a model, a symbol or a myth. It may be spelled out in mythical, anthropomorphic or pictorial terms, but its fundamental referent is the alleged *fact* that in Jesus of Nazareth, God, without ceasing to be God, became man.

There are two main problems with this doctrine, which

have led to its depreciation or abandonment in those strands of post-Enlightenment theology which I summarised just now. One concerns the rationality, intelligibility or coherence of the doctrine. The other concerns its historical basis, in the light of critical study of the New Testament. In this chapter I intend to say something about both of these problems, though more about the first than about the second. My examples are taken solely from Anglican theology in the last hundred years, partly because this chapter is intended as an Anglican contribution to ecumenical theology, and partly because the doctrine of the Incarnation has been a leading and characteristic strand in Anglican theology during this period. It is also very much at the centre of discussion at the present time as a result of the publication in the summer of 1977 of the controversial collection of essays, *The Myth of God Incarnate*. The shock which that book caused in Anglican circles is largely due to the centrality of incarnational theology in Anglicanism.

Before going on to discuss the substantial issues of the intelligibility of and historical basis for the doctrine of the Incarnation, I shall attempt a sketch of the main stages and themes in the Anglican discussion of the topic. The starting-point for a study of Anglican theology of the Incarnation in the modern period is generally regarded to be the publication of *Lux Mundi* in 1889.[1] This collection of essays was edited by Charles Gore, at that time Principal of Pusey House, Oxford. The book's subtitle indicated its theme: 'A Series of Studies in the Religion of the Incarnation'. Gore himself devoted the Bampton Lectures for 1891 to the same theme, *The Incarnation of the Son of God*.[2] His treatment of the doctrine, with its emphasis on the so-called kenotic theory, where our Lord's human knowledge was concerned, was one way in which the writers of the 'Lux mundi' school tried to relate their understanding of classical Christian doctrine to new knowledge. We shall discuss the kenotic theory below, and see some reason to question its adequacy. But there is no reason

55

to doubt Gore's intention, to restate orthodox Christian doctrine in the light of modern historical and philosophical thinking. The judgement of Don Cupitt in *The Myth of God Incarnate* that Gore was moving 'away from Chalcedonian orthodoxy' and that 'the last really able defence of a fully orthodox doctrine of Christ in Britain was H. P. Liddon's *The Divinity of Our Lord and Saviour Jesus Christ*'[3] is thoroughly tendentious, as I hope to show, and as indeed this whole period of Anglican theology will for the most part show. It is one of the fallacies of our contemporary liberals that there are no alternatives lying between the Christology of H. P. Liddon, for whom the Incarnate one was both human and omniscient, and their own non-incarnational Christology.

In the period between the publication of *Lux Mundi* and the First World War, in addition to Gore's Bampton Lectures and their sequel, *Dissertations on Subjects Connected with the Incarnation*,[4] a number of important studies appeared, including two by other contributors to *Lux Mundi*. J. R. Illingworth's *Personality Human and Divine*[5] showed the strong influence of philosophical idealism, but, despite the emphasis on divine immanence, Illingworth laboured hard (in John Macquarrie's words) 'to maintain the uniqueness of the incarnation in Christ'.[6] It has been observed that Anglican writers on the Incarnation have betrayed a tendency to discuss and emphasise the doctrine of the Incarnation by itself, apart from its connection with the doctrine of the Atonement, and there is a strand in Anglican theology, including Bishop Westcott in the nineteenth century and Austin Farrer in the twentieth, who have advanced the Scotist thesis that the Incarnation would have taken place in any case, irrespective of the fallen state of man. But another important strand in Anglican Christology has upheld the close connection between incarnation and atonement. We see this in the great work by R. C. Moberly, another contributor to *Lux Mundi*, entitled *Atonement and Personality*.[7]

A somewhat peculiar Christology was adumbrated by the well-known Oxford New-Testament scholar, William Sanday. In his *Christologies Ancient and Modern*[8] he sketched the tentative view that the locus of Christ's divinity lay in his subconscious, as it were subliminally controlling its human expression at the level of conscious life. There is very little to be said for this view, but it does represent a rather crude attempt to relate the doctrine of the Incarnation to a further important element in modern knowledge, the new psychology. Sanday quoted, with approval, another, and in fact much better, Anglican contribution that had appeared three years before, namely, *The One Christ* by Frank Weston,[9] shortly to become Bishop of Zanzibar. Although Weston rejected extreme kenoticism, it is possible to regard his treatment of the self-restraint of the divine Logos in living and acting through manhood at each stage of Jesus' life as one of the best and most morally convincing statements of the kenotic view.

The attempt to restate the classical doctrine of the Incarnation in the light of modern knowledge and contemporary philosophy continued to characterise Anglican theology during and after the first World War. H. M. Relton's *A Study in Christology*[10] was a resolute defence of the doctrine of 'enhypostasia', as adumbrated by Leontius of Byzantium and John of Damascus. The influential churchman and theologian, William Temple, had been highly critical of the Chalcedonian formula in the essay which he contributed to *Foundations*,[11] but in *Christus Veritas*[12] he withdrew much of his criticism and presented a broadly orthodox Christology within a general metaphysical framework which was already moving from his earlier idealism to his later 'dialectical realism', as he called it, in which the Incarnation is regarded as the culmination of what, in the light of its highest level, spirit, we see to be an evolving sacramental universe. Temple's forthright criticisms of kenotic Christology have often been quoted, but, as J. M. Creed points out in his essay in

57

Mysterium Christi,[13] Temple himself appears to be unable to avoid at least implicit use of the kenotic principle. Lionel Thornton's *The Incarnate Lord*[14] made use of a rather different philosophical system, namely the philosophy of organism of Alfred North Whitehead. The interest of Temple's and Thornton's work, whatever criticisms we may wish to make of their philosophical standpoints, is that it illustrates the possibility of restating the classical doctrines of Creation and Incarnation in terms of a dynamic evolutionary conception of the world process. The attempt to relate Christology to the new psychology reappears in L. W. Grensted's *The Person of Christ*.[15]

The authors mentioned so far, from Gore to Grensted, were all concerned to express the classical faith of Christendom in the light of modern historical and scientific knowledge and philosophical speculation. But we must now retrace our steps and refer to a quite different and less typical strand in Anglican theology, very much influenced by German liberal Protestantism, whose Christology can roughly be described as non-incarnational. Already in 1914, when Frank Weston issued a second edition of *The One Christ*, he added a Preface about 'the Modernism of Liberal Churchmen'. But this type of Christology came into widespread public notice in England only with the Girton Conference of the Modern Churchmen's Union in 1921. It would be unfair to accuse theologians such as Hastings Rashdall and J. F. Bethune-Baker of wishing to deny the divinity of Christ, or of being unwilling to use in some sense the concept of incarnation; but the manner in which they found themselves restating the doctrine of Christ reveals an undeniable break with classical Christian doctrine and justifies the term 'non-incarnational'. Thus Rashdall wrote:

We can form no higher conception of God than we see exhibited in humanity at its highest, and in Christ, as in no other man before or since, we may see what humanity at its highest is, and therefore in Him we believe that God has made a full and sufficient revelation of Himself. His character is the character of God. In Him God is once and for all revealed.[16]

And Bethune-Baker wrote: 'God stands to me for the highest values in life, and because I believe those values were actualised in the person and life of Jesus, I must use the title ''God'' of him', and 'when I say that the man Jesus is ''God'', I mean that he is for me the index of my conception of God'.[17] The question of the adequacy of such views as these was much discussed in the 1920s and 30s. We find in addition to Temple and Thornton characteristically Anglican writers such as J. K. Mozley and O. C. Quick, less wedded to a particular philosophical framework, yet flexible and self-critical in their appropriation of the classical Christian tradition. Both were fundamentally opposed to liberal Protestantism and to the kind of position which came to expression in the Girton Conference of 1921. Mozley was the more 'Catholic' of the two. He contributed an essay on 'The Incarnation' to *Essays Catholic and Critical*[18] and another on 'Christology and Soteriology' to *Mysterium Christi*, the latter constituting an admirable statement of the way in which it is soteriological considerations that require us to think of Jesus as coming to the world from the side of God, and not as the highest stage of religious evolution. Mozley's *The Doctrine of the Incarnation*,[19] although a small book, represents further his balanced and perceptive understanding of classical Christianity. Oliver Quick was the more philosophical mind, and in a series of short books, from *Modern Philosophy and the Incarnation* up to *Doctrines of the Creed*,[20] and again in his sadly unpublished lectures on Christology (1941/2), he devoted much space to the careful articulation of an incarnational Christology. His treatment of kenoticism and of the impossibility of maintaining the patristic concept of divine impassibility are among the most careful which these topics have received. Quick said of Bethune-Baker's position that it represented a reversal of classical Christology; for it made Jesus' 'divinity' a predicate of his humanity.

59

Quick, Mozley, Grensted, Thornton and Temple were all members of the Church of England Doctrine Commission, which was in part set up in the wake of the Girton Conference controversies, and which published in 1938 a much-discussed report entitled *Doctrine in the Church of England*.[21] It is significant that while this report recognises a broad range of views on Christology (and on other subjects) as permissible within the Church of England, this range does not include what I have called the non-incarnational Christology of many contributors to the Girton Conference of 1921. In so far as the 1938 report can be thought of as a summing up of Anglican theology, it is clear that that theology remained firmly incarnational. Even J. M. Creed, another member of the Doctrine Commission, whose knowledge of German theology was as great as any Anglican of that time, and who certainly wished to be thought of as a Modern Churchman, revealed in his *The Divinity of Jesus Christ*,[22] published in the same year, an appreciation of the fact that the doctrine of the cosmic Christ necessarily takes the Christian theologian beyond the position of Rashdall and Bethune-Baker.

Leonard Hodgson was another Anglican theologian who, like Mozley and Quick, endeavoured to explore and state the rationality of classical Christian doctrine. He contributed an essay on 'The Incarnation' to A. E. J. Rawlinson's collection, *Essays on the Trinity and the Incarnation*,[23] and dealt with Christology in many of his books.[24] The question which Hodgson asked of the apostolic and patristic writings, namely, 'What must the truth have been if it appeared like this to men who thought like that?', has often been quoted, and typifies his approach.

The position of theologians such as Mozley, Quick and Hodgson can be described as 'critical orthodoxy', and it is the lack of such figures in the period since the Second World War that constitutes one of the signal weaknesses of contemporary Anglicanism. It is true that Hodgson was still writing in the

1950s, and the name of W. R. Matthews, whose *The Problem of Christ in the Twentieth Century* appeared in 1950,[25] could be added to this list. But the Church of England's most prolific living author, E. L. Mascall, is, for the most part, an untypical figure, in that his christological writings are largely based on the very interesting contributions of French Roman Catholic writers.[26] Only the philosophical theologian Austin Farrer, who, sadly, wrote little on doctrinal topics, but whose careful and reflective grasp of classical Christian doctrine can be gathered from his many occasional writings and sermons,[27] maintained into the 1960s the tradition of Mozley, Quick and Hodgson.[28] Apart from John Macquarrie, whose *Principles of Christian Theology*[29] represents a bold attempt to use Heideggerian ontology in the articulation of Christian doctrine, the most common approach to Christology in recent Anglican writing has been along the lines of the Presbyterian scholar D. M. Baillie's well-known book, *God Was In Christ*.[30] Thus in articles in the collections *Soundings* and *Christ For Us Today*,[31] H. W. Montefiore advances the view that talk of God's action in Christ is more appropriate than that of 'being'. Similarly John Robinson, in *The Human Face of God*,[32] wishes to endorse the view that Christ's divinity consisted in what God did in him. I shall have something to say below about the suggestion that the concept of 'activity' can replace that of 'being' in fundamental Christology, but it seems evident that this approach in fact was a highly insecure one; for we find that these tendencies in current Anglican theology have led to the reappearance of a much more extreme form of liberal Protestantism even than that of the Girton Conference of 1921. Thus we find the Regius Professors of Divinity at Oxford and at Cambridge explicitly rejecting the doctrine of the Incarnation, Professor Maurice Wiles in *The Remaking of Christian Doctrine*[33] and in his contributions to *The Myth of God Incarnate*, and Professor Geoffrey Lampe in his Bampton Lectures, *God as Spirit*.[34]

This powerful advocacy of what amounts to unitarianism in contemporary Anglican theology drives us back to a re-examination of the propriety of the doctrine of the Incarnation for Christology today.[35]

It should be stressed at the beginning that the argument for the propriety of the doctrine of the Incarnation for Christology today has both a negative and a positive pole. Negatively, it needs to be shown how it is dissatisfaction with liberal or modernist versions of Christology that drives us back to classical incarnational Christology. Positively, we need to do three things – first, to spell out the morally and religiously compelling nature of the doctrine of the Incarnation, then, secondly and thirdly, to meet the two conditions mentioned earlier, namely, that of showing the rationality and coherence of the doctrine, and that of indicating its basis (in part, but only in part, its historical basis) in the relevant evidence.

Dissatisfaction with non-incarnational Christologies has often taken the form of questioning the adequacy of the purely human Jesus, however God-conscious and however inspired by God, to sustain the doctrine of Atonement. Thus Mozley pointed out that wherever the soteriological motive appeared, Jesus could be thought of only as coming to the world from the side of God; and Hodgson pointed out that an objective doctrine of Atonement, that is to say, one which posits universal significance in the Christ event for the reconciliation of man and God, requires us to see the Cross as an act of God incarnate. But the implausibility of the liberal account of Jesus is greater than this. It is not only a question of the weakness of liberal Christology *vis-à-vis* atonement theory. There is a more general weakness regarding the sense that can be made of the idea that God was able at one point in time to win the pure and unbroken response of a particular individual man two thousand years ago, and nowhere else before or since. The weakness of exemplarist theories of atonement is not just their subjective nature. It is much more their inability to account for the absoluteness of the example. This weakness stands out very clearly in the Bampton Lectures of Professor Lampe. He speaks of Jesus' response to God as 'uniquely perfect and unbroken', but there is no theology of incarnation to account for the possibility of such perfection, especially in the light of Lampe's conviction that all human media of divine action are fallible, and that in fact the followers of Jesus have radically misunderstood him almost from the start.

Much more plausible, actually, on non-incarnational premises, is the modernist position, which admits that we can have no historical basis for predicating perfection of Jesus anyway, and which tends towards the relativist view of the Jesus tradition as one channel among others in world religion for the fostering of human spiritual experience. The suggestion that there is no easy resting place between incarnational Christology, which at least explains both the perfection and the cosmic significance of Jesus Christ and the extreme modernist and relativist Christology, which turns Jesus into one guru among others, should send us back to the positive case for incarnational Christology.

Before examining its rationality, I should like to say something about its morally and religiously compelling nature. For there can be no doubt that a large part of the attraction and force of the Christian gospel down the ages, in the minds of simple believers and theologians alike, has been the conviction that God is not a remote and vague transcendent X, to be propitiated or worshipped in fear or ecstasy, but a God who, out of his great love, has made himself known personally by coming amongst us as one of us, so that the character, acts and teaching of Jesus, and in particular his passion and death, are seen as God's own revelatory and loving acts for our salvation. Of course the transcendent X of theistic religion the world over has been filled out in many different ways by conceptions of God as creator (and destroyer), as supreme spirit, as sovereign will, making his law and reality known through prophets and sages. He has been conceived of as loving provider of those who turn to him, and indeed as Lord of a chosen people and as one who acts in history. In the theistic traditions of world religion, God is not just the transcendent source of the world's being and value. He is immanent in mystical experience, moral awareness and historical providence. In mystical experience, indeed, the immanence is sometimes even thought of as identity. But the special force of Christian belief has always been the uniquely personal nature of God's self-revelation in the person and fate of Jesus. Moreover, if the suffering and Cross of Jesus can be seen as God's own suffering and Cross in the world, then we have a much more morally powerful and credible conception of God than one which postulates divine revelation solely through a representative or series of representatives. The revelatory and moral force of the belief that God wins our love by coming as a servant and by 'loving his own to the end' is very great. In particular, it is the manner in which our God is believed to have taken upon himself the burden of the world's evil that renders him morally credible. For Christian belief, God takes responsibility for the suffering and evil entailed in creation by making himself vulnerable to it and by himself experiencing its pain and dereliction. Moreover the trinitarian conception of God, which belief in the Incarnation implies, is a much more religiously fertile conception of God than that of undifferentiated monotheism. Not only is the relation between the man Jesus and his heavenly Father held to mirror for us the internal relation of love given and love received within the deity, but we too, in our prayers and worship, are caught up into the trinitarian life of God by the Spirit at work in our hearts. Our worship is literally inspired, not only from without, but from within.

The intelligibility of such conceptions has come under sustained attack in the tradition of liberal Protestantism, as exemplified in much recent Anglican and other writing. I shall concentrate attention here on criticism of the concept of 'incarnation', namely that it is self-contradictory to speak of one who is both God and man. It is not sufficient to point out, as I have done elsewhere,[36] that the suggestion of straight contradiction is easily avoided by recognition of the fact that we are not talking about precisely defined concepts such as 'circle' and 'square', where the definitions are immediately seen to be incompatible. Certainly 'God' and 'man' are not so precisely defined, least of all the former; and unless we build into our conception of God an appropriate measure of agnosticism, we shall find ourselves talking about something quite other than God. In theology, we have to learn what cannot as well as what can be said. But the coherence of talk about one who is 'very God and very man' must be defended much more positively than by reference to divine incomprehensibility, however essential an element in Christian theism that is – as the Greek Fathers well knew. Something must be said about the positive grounds for thinking that God is such as to be able, in one of the modes of his being, without ceasing to be God, to take human nature into himself and come amongst us as one of us. On the one hand, then, we need to spell out the trinitarian nature of God, whereby it becomes conceivable that the infinite, yet internally differentiated deity, can live out a real human life from a centre in himself, and relate himself to himself in the manner in which we read of the prayers of Jesus to the Father. On the other hand, we need to point out that humanity, made in the image of God, is not alien to its personal Creator. In a sermon on 'Incarnation', Austin Farrer pointed out that the admittedly paradoxical notion of deity living out the life of a freelance rabbi is not the sheer nonsense of the supposition that God might have become incarnate in an unreasoning beast. 'Deity is reasonable mind', he said, 'and cannot express himself personally through anything else; not, therefore, through an unreasoning creature.' By contrast with that nonsensical idea 'the incarnation of God in a man makes sense; finite mind or person becomes the vehicle of infinite mind, infinite person'.[37]

Farrer insists that, far from our concept of God ruling out the possibility of incarnation, it is the doctrine of the Incarnation that defines the Christian concept of God. On this reckoning, God *must* be such as to be able, without ceasing to be God, to express himself through a human life. To suppose that the life of Jesus was lived out from a centre in deity is in no way to deny the genuine humanity of Jesus. The idea that such a 'high' Christology is inevitably docetic represents a poverty of both imagination and theological grasp; for the whole point of the doctrine of the Incarnation is that here God makes himself known in and through a real human life at each stage of human growth and knowledge. Thus Farrer writes of God, out of his great love, accepting every circumstance of our manhood. 'He spared himself nothing', Farrer goes on. 'He was not a copybook man-in-general, he was a Galilean carpenter, a free-lance rabbi; and he wove up his life, as each of us must, out of the materials that were to hand.'[38]

This leads us naturally to consider the degree to which our recognition of the humanity of Christ (the human limitations, that is, of his knowledge and self-knowledge) compels us to adopt some form of kenotic Christology. Nineteenth-century kenotic Christology was rightly criticised for its metaphysical naivety; for we cannot seriously suppose that the Incarnation involved an abandonment of divine attributes or a depotentiation of the Logos. On the contrary, it lies at the heart of Christianity to suppose that God's omnipotence was both exercised and revealed in his becoming man, subjecting himself to human limitations, and dying a cruel death. Moreover that humanity and that human experience are believed to have been permanently taken into the being of God. The

Incarnation was not a temporary episode. On the other hand, we are bound to say that this personal presence and activity of God this side of the gap between Creator and creature necessarily involved an appropriate self-limitation and self-restraint. We may well say that in all his relations with his temporal creation, the eternal God limits himself appropriately and relates himself to the world in a manner appropriate to its finite temporality. (There is room here for rethinking the notion of divine omniscience *vis-à-vis* the not yet existent future of a world of open possibilities.) Even more so in incarnation are we to suppose that God in one of the modes of his being (which we call the Word or Son) limited himself by living out a human life, involving genuine growth, limited knowledge and a restricted conceptual horizon. *Qua* incarnate he shared, for example, the demonological and apocalyptic horizon of first-century Palestinian Judaism, and conceived of his mission in terms fashioned from contemporary Jewish expectation. It is highly implausible for us, in the light of informed and critical study of the New Testament, as well as of philosophical and psychological realism about what it is to be a man, to suppose that Jesus knew himself to be or thought of himself as divine. In Austin Farrer's words, 'An omniscient being cannot be very man. But he knew *how* to be the Son of God in the several situations of his gradually unfolding destiny. God the Son on earth is a fullness of holy life within the limit of mortality.'[39] Some element of kenotic theory must undoubtedly be called upon to give an account, as far as human language permits, of this paradoxical fact of a genuinely human life lived out from a centre in deity.

There is no doubt that it is primarily modern historical knowledge that encourages us to think in these terms, and it is not surprising that kenotic Christology is largely a nineteenth- and twentieth-century affair. But it is an arbitrary stipulation to declare that orthodoxy cannot embrace this consequent rethinking of the implications of the doctrine of the

Incarnation and its significance. I think here particularly of O. C. Quick's repeatedly expressed conviction that the concept of divine impassibility required radical re-examination in the light of the Incarnation.

The moral force of kenotic Christology has long been appreciated. But our recognition of the self-limitation of the Son of God involved in his becoming man should not lead us to draw inappropriate conclusions where the divinity is concerned. Something was clearly wrong with the theological thinking of William Temple, when he pressed the question against kenoticism: 'What was happening to the rest of the universe during the period of our Lord's earthly life?'.[40] We cannot present kenotic Christology in such a way as to imply the abandonment of the divine functions of the Logos. On the contrary, we have to add to the 'et incarnatus est' the qualifying phrase 'without ceasing to be God'. Moreover we have to suppose that while the man Jesus in his earthly life was presumably unaware of his divinity, the Blessed Trinity was perfectly well aware of what was being done, experienced and suffered. This is not to attribute two consciousnesses to *Jesus*. But it is to assert that the consciousness of the man Jesus was the limited human expression of the omniscient divine consciousness. God, *qua* God, knew what he was doing; *qua* man he learned obedience like any other Jewish child. Similarly we do not predicate two wills of the man Jesus. But his human will, perfectly dedicated to do his heavenly Father's will, was nevertheless the earthly expression of the divine will. There is thus a sense in which we must speak of two consciousnesses and two wills, just as we must speak of two natures; but such language tends to break down when we think too anthropomorphically of the divine consciousness, will or nature as alongside of and comparable to the human consciousness, will or nature of Jesus. It is at this point that we must remember that we are struggling to speak of the infinite, internally differentiated, being of God, whose own eternal love, given and received within the Trinity, is mirrored in the love of Jesus for the Father, that human love being expressed in categories of thought and action provided by the faith of Israel in which he grew up.

We do not *have* to express the conviction that God, in one of the modes of his being, without in any way ceasing to be God, became man, in the technical language of substance, nature and hypostasis. But neither can we afford to reject the Chalcedonian formula. Such language may evoke inappropriate connotations in our minds, but we cannot avoid some way of expressing in ontological terms the identity between Jesus and the Logos, which the doctrine of the Incarnation asserts, and which Chalcedon tried to safeguard.

I pointed out that much Anglican Christology since the Second World War has attempted to replace the category of 'substance' with that of 'action' and to rest content with talk of what God 'did' in Christ. This suggestion can be countered in two ways. On the one hand it can be pointed out that the difference between liberal and orthodox Christology can itself be put in terms of 'action'. It is the difference between the view that God 'acted' supremely through the man Jesus and the view that the human life and death of Jesus were supremely God's own 'act' for our salvation. On the other hand, if we adopt the latter view, what I call the 'orthodox' view, that the life of Jesus was God's own act here in our midst, we shall soon find ourselves driven to spell out the ontology of the situation in language not unlike that of 'substance'. To say that the acts of Jesus *were* the acts of God incarnate is to assert the 'homo-ousion'. The propriety of such use of 'substance' in Christology has been defended in recent essays by two Cambridge Anglicans, Professors Donald MacKinnon and Christopher Stead.[41]

The term 'hypostasis' is much more difficult to handle. There is no doubt that early attempts to state the relation between the divinity and humanity of Christ were crude and unsatisfactory. We cannot suppose that the divine Logos took the place of some element in the human being of Jesus. If we are to subscribe positively to the doctrine of 'enhypostasia' and hold that the human life of Jesus was lived out from a centre in deity, and negatively to the doctrine of 'anhypostasia' and hold that Jesus was not independently a merely human subject, these doctrines must not be taken to imply that Jesus lacked a human mind, will, consciousness or personality. But they do imply that the metaphysical subject of the human life of Jesus was the eternal Son of God, and that we cannot think of the man Jesus apart from his being God incarnate.

The implications of the doctrine of the Incarnation, so understood, are very great. For our understanding of God, they are the starting-point of trinitarian thinking. We are to construe the personal relation between the man Jesus and his heavenly Father as the incarnate expression of the eternal relation subsisting between the Son and the Father. By contrast the relation between the divinity and the humanity of Christ is not itself a personal relation or even a relation at all. It is a matter of identity. Jesus *is* the incarnate Son. For our understanding of the relation between God and the world, the implications of the doctrine of the Incarnation are equally far reaching. It means that we are not to conceive of the immanence of the transcendent God in his creation as uniform throughout history. On the contrary, creation and history are to be thought of as pivoted around the unique span of space–time in which the incarnate life was lived. The Incarnation was not a bolt from the blue that might have happened anywhere or at any time. In order to be the vehicle of divine life in our midst, the humanity of Jesus in all its contextual and relational ramifications had to be prepared for through centuries of providential action in history. Similarly it is in relation to the risen and ascended Christ that the subsequent history of humanity finds its ultimate fulfilment in God.

At this point something should be said not only about the

post-existence but also about the pre-existence of Christ. The relation between eternity and time is hard to discuss from our standpoint of inescapable practical and conceptual involvement in the temporal process. We should in any case have to question the traditional interpretation of eternity as timelessness, but whatever we may say about the eternal temporality of God, we shall unquestionably need to speak of the relation between God and his temporally structured creation in temporal terms. I have already suggested that this reflects an aspect of God's self-limitation in creation, irrespective of incarnation. But incarnation clearly involves a further and closer mode of identification on God's part with the created, temporally structured world. If indeed the human life of Jesus Christ is lived out from a centre in God, then we shall need to speak of his pre-existence. For that centre in God must be thought of as ontologically and temporally (we are speaking of God's temporality here) prior to his incarnate life. The pre-existence of Christ is therefore the 'pre-existence' of God the Son. It is not the pre-existence of the humanity of the man Jesus; for the incarnate life had a beginning in time (our time). No doubt that particular slice of space–time in which the life of Jesus here on earth was located represents the outworking through divine providence of the eternal intention of God to relate himself to his creation in this way. To speak of the 'lamb slain before the foundation of the world' is, I presume, to speak very graphically of this intention and, of course, of the fact that the Cross is indeed *God*'s Cross in our world.

The question of the post-existence of Christ is different. Of course, the fundamental subject remains the same – God, in that mode or centre of his being that we call the Word or Son – but Christ is risen. The risen and ascended Christ is God the Son permanently expressed and focused for us through his incarnate humanity. Here and in God's 'future', we do not cease to find our fulfilment in relation to God made man.

One further difficulty in the doctrine of the Incarnation needs to be considered here. I spoke of the implausibility of the picture of Jesus' perfect human life as still maintained in liberal, non-incarnational Christology; and indeed it seems that the doctrine of the sinlessness of Christ is a theological postulate deduced from the doctrine of the Incarnation rather than an inference from historical evidence. Admittedly, it is not easy to distinguish interpretation and fact here, and it could be argued that the historical facts *must* have been such as to be capable of sustaining the post-Easter tradition. Certainly the Jesus of the Gospels, unlike the greatest saints, shows no sign of a sense of unworthiness nor of any need for penitence. But, of course, the Gospels are written out of the 'high' Christological faith of the early communities. Even so, the point against liberal Protestant, non-incarnational Christologies holds: if the life of Jesus was a 'perfect and unbroken response' to his heavenly Father, this could only have been because his human life was lived out of a centre in God. (There is no reason to suppose that this protected him from profound experience of temptation, but it is sheer romanticism to suppose that 'peccability' is of the essence of human nature, and that the whole God–man relation was really put at risk in the Incarnation. The freedom of Jesus, we must suppose, was always exercised in conformity with the Father's will, just because the human freedom was the vehicle of the divine freedom.)

It needs to be stressed once more what is lost if we cease to think in incarnational terms and rest content with the view that God *simpliciter* made himself known through the man Jesus by inspiration. We lose the peculiarly moral and personal force of the belief that 'for us men and for our salvation' the eternal Son 'came down from heaven', that God's love was enacted here in our midst, that God himself took upon himself both responsibility for and the burden of the world's evil. We lose the religious force of the belief that we are ourselves caught up into the trinitarian life of God, as, in the Spirit and by sacrament, we are confronted by the risen Christ and adopted into his mystical body. These are, after all, the distinctive features of specifically Christian faith in God.

Having said something to indicate the rationality and force of Christian incarnational belief, I must add a few remarks about its factual basis. For not only is the intelligibility of the doctrine challenged in recent liberal and modernist writing, but also its claim to rest secure upon the historical evidence of the New Testament. It cannot be claimed that Anglican theology in the twentieth century has grappled with this problem with the thoroughness and pertinacity of our continental colleagues. One thinks only of A. E. J. Rawlinson's *The New Testament Doctrine of Christ*,[42] and of E. Hoskyns and N. Davey's *The Riddle of the New Testament*.[43] But one has to admit that the tradition so ably represented in post-Second World War Anglican New Testament studies by Professor C. F. D. Moule's book *The Origins of Christology*[44] has more in common with the free church tradition of T. W. Manson, Vincent Taylor and C. H. Dodd than anything characteristically Anglican. It is well known how all these scholars retained a basic confidence in the historical reliability of the New Testament documents at a time when their German colleagues, for the most part, professed a considerable degree of historical skepticism. (It is remarkable that the alleged gulf between the 'Jesus of history' and the 'Christ of faith' is being asserted again in some Anglican quarters just when it is being subjected to searching criticism in Germany itself.) But it is quite understandable that Anglican theologians have not been disposed to investigate the doctrine of the Incarnation on the basis of New Testament study alone. For they have, for the most part, worked within the framework of a doctrine of the Church that has disposed them to think of the tradition of faith as continuous with its foundations in the events to which the New Testament as a whole, not just the Gospels, bears witness. This sense of living within the Body of Christ, for all its empirical faults, has predisposed the Anglican mind to take the theological tradition of creeds and Councils as itself under the divine providence. Not that the human media of faith's transmission are thought to be without errors or without the deficiencies of particular cultural conceptualisation. The doctrine of providence does not involve the preclusion of error, but it does suggest that, despite human error and limitation, God's will is done, and that it is unlikely that the Church's self-understanding down the centuries has been as radically mistaken as some liberals and modernists suppose. I dare say that it is some such understanding of the Church as the body of the living Christ that enabled Austin Farrer, for one, to expound the traditional doctrine with great faithfulness and insight (yet with due regard to the hermeneutical problem of translation), while at the same time speculating somewhat fancifully on the biblical material itself, employing techniques which some of his pupils, having lost Farrer's sense of the doctrinal tradition, now bend to liberal purposes.

For 'critical orthodoxy', New Testament criticism is not only to be respected and used for its own sake as a necessary historical discipline. It is also important theologically in that it forces us to take more seriously than ever before the genuine humanity of Christ. It is no longer possible to defend the divinity of Christ by reference to the claims of Jesus. But more than this, it is seen to be theologically inappropriate to suppose that the divinity overrode the humanity and asserted itself in ways which strain psychological and historical credibility. We may still wish to say that the divinity was manifest in the humanity; but this is not an impartial historical judgement. It is said only with hindsight, in the light of the resurrection and of the spiritual and sacramental experience of Christians ever since. Of course the rapid

The propriety of the doctrine of the Incarnation

growth of 'high' Christologies in Paul and John and the other New-Testament writers is itself a historical fact requiring explanation; but it is implausible to suppose that a critical reconstruction of the historical Jesus will ever be sufficient by itself to account for the rise of Christianity and for experience of life in the body of Christ. Not that, on a purely historical reconstruction, Jesus appears as no more than a typical Jewish rabbi of the first century. Justice must be done to the unique and remarkable facts of his life and teaching, the authority with which he spoke, his effect on those with whom he came into contact, the way in which he took upon himself the eschatological expectations of the Jews, and the way in which he went to his death. It was no ordinary man who was raised from the dead. To put the matter theologically, whatever degree of kenoticism we accept, and even if the divine nature was not present to Jesus' own human self-consciousness, we cannot suppose that the human vehicle of the divine presence totally obscured the real identity of the incarnate one. The divinity, we may say with hindsight, showed itself in the humanity.

Clearly, on this interpretation, a purely historical reconstruction of the life of Jesus of Nazareth, while it will undoubtedly contain puzzling and remarkable features, will not be sufficient by itself to create or sustain belief in the divinity of Christ. But it must at least be compatible with such an interpretation, and even, as I have argued, be sufficient to suggest it, when scrutinised with hindsight, in the light of the Easter faith.

In *Doctrines of the Creed*,[45] O. C. Quick discussed the different presuppositions of the believer and of the critic regarding the bearing of historical criticism on the doctrine of the Incarnation. It is typical of this writer and of the tradition of 'critical orthodoxy' which he represented and which I have tried to defend and carry forward in this paper, to be explicit about this matter. Quick points out that while Christians do not deny the duty nor prejudge the results of critical investigation, they are bound to assess those results in the light of the faith by which they live. That faith itself, as we have said, is not a rigid structure. To come to accept an element of kenoticism in one's Christology is in part the effect of critical investigation. But kenotic Christology itself will predispose the believer to judge the evidence more positively than does the historian who sees no particular value in the doctrine. The believer, by contrast, is impressed by the effects of the Christ event, effects in which he himself participates and finds meaning. 'The defence of the Christian's convictions about the historical origins of his faith', said Quick, 'will always rest mainly upon the principle that effects must have an adequate cause.'

7

The Church and Christology

Recent disputes over the doctrine of the Incarnation give rise to the following questions. Does it make a difference to our reflection on the person and work of Christ if we carry out that reflection as participating members of the Church – as self-consciously Church theologians? And, if it does make a difference, what difference does it make? Two further questions also arise. Ought it to make a difference? And are these appropriate or even proper questions to ask? The Church theologian, furthermore, is bound to consider the practical problem of the Church's attitude or policy towards what is widely felt to be heterodox or deviant theology in its midst.

Consideration of these questions may be prefaced by a summary of the main objections to be levelled against the kind of non-incarnational Christology advocated in *The Myth of God Incarnate*. In the first place may be mentioned intellectual dissatisfaction over the intelligibility of an interpretation of Jesus simply as a human vehicle of divine grace and revelation. It seems hard to account for the unique or even special status of Jesus in these terms – a difficulty glaringly apparent in the Bampton Lectures of Geoffrey Lampe, *God as Spirit*. It seems much more logical on that basis to relativise Jesus much more thoroughly as one great saint or prophet or religious innovator among others. On such a view, of course, one's departure from both scripture and tradition is all the more blatant. Secondly, there is the objection that accusations of incoherence levelled at the Chalcedonian Definition and at the doctrines of the creeds are much too crude and insensitive. The reductionists appear to be attacking caricatures and men of straw, and expending no effort to see what talk of God made man or of one who is *vere Deus et vere homo* might mean. Thirdly, there is suspicion of the criterion of economy advocated by Maurice Wiles,[1] whereby only what is demanded or required by the historical evidence is to be retained as acceptable Christian doctrine. This objection will be developed in what follows, since the main concern of this essay is to examine the proper framework within which these only partly historical matters are to be judged. In the fourth place we must be quite clear about what is lost from Christianity if we take the non-incarnational path. It is in this connection that the moral and religious significance of the doctrine of the Incarnation needs to be spelled out. This may be done under five heads: (a) the significance of Christ for our personal knowledge of God, when Christ is believed to be God made man; (b) the consequential relational, trinitarian, understanding of God to which incarnational belief gives rise – at stake here is the basic Christian affirmation that God *is* Love in his own eternal being, irrespective of his love for us; (c) the significance of the Cross as God's own subjection of himself, in one of the modes of his being, to pain and suffering and death – here we are speaking both of an adequate theology of atonement and of the problem of theodicy; (d) the significance of Christ as a living presence, with whom Christian people are in communion today and in whom they are one with all Christians, the dead and the living, in his Body, the Church and in the Communion of Saints; and (e) the eschatological dimension – whether it is true that, in the end, it is in Christ that we shall finally be united with the Father.

Not all these points will be developed here. The focus of attention in this chapter is whether the Church theologian begs the question by claiming to do his theology on the basis of participation in the Body of Christ, or whether that participation in fact gives him the only proper perspective from which to judge these matters – including the historical evidence.

Certainly it makes a difference whether he approaches the critical study of scripture and tradition simply as an individual scholar, subjecting the variegated data to scrutiny according to the general criteria of literary and historical scholarship, or whether he carries out his critical investigations self-consciously as a Church theologian, reflecting on the origins and development of a movement in which he himself fully participates and finds meaningful and indeed normative for his interpretation of reality and experience as a whole. I am not suggesting that the Church theologian should ignore the general criteria of literary and historical scholarship. The suggestion is rather that their use within a different total framework of approach may well yield different overall results.

Recent critics of incarnational Christology give the impression of approaching these questions in an extremely individualistic and piecemeal way. Biblical texts and patristic texts are scrutinised not only irrespective of what, as a matter of fact, has emerged from them, but also on the basis of a strict effort at non-participatory objectivity. This raises the question, can doctrinal truth be attained that way? In considering the historical questions we must surely take account both of what has emerged from those beginnings and of at least the possible framework of interpretation provided by participation in the community that lives by that tradition. New presumably someone who lives by that tradition is someone who finds the doctrines of the Church religiously and morally compelling. Of course there is room for critical revaluation of the faith as it has been understood so far. The theologian's – and indeed the Christian's – understanding of the faith must undoubtedly be a growing, developing thing. No plea is being made here for infallibility in the development of Christian doctrine. But it is not unreasonable to ask whether the great christological and soteriological doctrines that were wrestled over in the patristic age, in medieval times, in the Reformation and counter-Reformation, and then, in their various ways, in modern times, are really to be dismissed as aspects of some monumental misunderstanding of the nature and significance of Jesus. At least it needs to be asked whether such a radical reassessment of the Christian tradition is compatible with genuinely Church theology.

These questions may be pursued a little further in respect of two problems, one doctrinal, the other historical. The first concerns the dispute between Christology 'from above' and Christology 'from below'. These are very confusing slogans; for clearly all Christology is from below in that it is a branch of theology undertaken by human beings. God does not write Christology books. But of course the slogans 'from above' and 'from below' are designed to mark the contrast between those who base their Christology on the man Jesus of Nazareth and those who base it on God's own being and acts in revelation and incarnation. But even here the distinction is not clear-cut. For it may be thought wise (or indeed essential) to begin from below, that is, with the man Jesus of Nazareth, and yet the enquiry may still lead us in the end to an understanding of Jesus as coming to us from the side of God, i.e. 'from above'. Only if one both begins and ends with Jesus the man does one's Christology remain thoroughly earthbound – 'from below' – throughout. The crucial question is this: what difference does it make if we approach this dispute as Church theologians reflecting on the basis of our own practice and worship as members of the Body of Christ and in communion and fellowship with that Body's Head? Clearly the disposition of the Church theologian will be to do Christology 'from above', to try to understand the meaning of the faith of the Church as it has been handed down through Councils and creeds and confessional statements. Admittedly the theologian will want to trace the origins and basis of the Church's faith in the events concerning Jesus. To that end he will wish to go back to the beginning and tell the story 'from below'. Indeed it is not only essential for apologetic purposes to do this, but the rationality of his own self-understanding as a Christian theologian depends upon his ability to make these connections. This point, incidentally, has much to do with our evaluation of the work of Schillebeeckx, about whom something will be said later in this chapter.

The Church theologian as such has no special interest in restricting his perspective to the purely human, in other words in remaining resolutely 'below'. Some modern theologians give the impression that unless they remain within the framework of purely human categories their talk of Jesus will make no contact with the mind of their contemporaries. But it is one thing to begin where other people are, quite another to remain there for fear of offending secular sensibilities. That is to betray a loss of confidence in the Church's tradition as a possible framework for the interpretation of reality.

Anyone who believes that the Christian religion stands or falls with the conviction that Jesus Christ comes to us from the side of God is bound to hold that Church Christology must in the end be Christology 'from above'. But there is no need to dismiss Christology 'from below' as an apologetic or justificatory method of substantiating the Church's faith and showing its origins in a real human life and fate. Indeed there are dangers of docetism and ideology and fantasy in ignoring the historical question and the real humanity of Jesus.

The second problem is the historical problem. What difference does it make to historical judgements about Jesus and the early Church when the matter is approached from a standpoint of membership and participation in the Christian body? This is undoubtedly a very delicate issue. C. F. D. Moule has been accused of reading the Church's doctrine into

the historical facts, instead of showing genuine continuity between Jesus and the Christ of faith, when, in his book *The
Origins of Christology*, he argues that the seeds of later
christological doctrine are there in the story of Jesus himself.
But the question arises whether the historical facts can
perhaps only be read aright, not only in the light of what has
actually developed from them, but in the light of the
theologian's own participation in and experience of the
Church and its faith. That faith must be critically appro-
priated, of course. Not any and every doctrinal development
can be justified. Moreover the hard historical work of tracing
origins and continuities has to be done. The kind of work that
C. F. D. Moule in England and M. Hengel in Germany are
doing has to be done well and subjected to the critical comment of other historians. It has to be shown to be a possible
reconstruction, by the standards of strict historical scholarship.
But when Maurice Wiles says that our doctrinal reconstruction
must be necessitated by the evidence, the question has to be
pressed, does he mean necessitated by the historical evidence
scrutinised in isolation from involvement in the Church, or
does he mean necessitated by the historical evidence together
with the data of experiential participation in the living Church
and rational reflection on the Church's doctrine from within?
Apparently he means the former – the purely historical
research, irrespective of Church membership – but it is far
from clear that that provides the right framework within which
to judge even the historical questions.

There is very good treatment of these problems in chapter
XIV of O. C. Quick's *Doctrines of the Creed*, the chapter
entitled 'The Incarnation and Historical Criticism'.[2] Quick
frankly points out here the different presuppositions of the
believer and the critic:

If the meaning of the Christian faith, involving certain beliefs about
the historical life of Jesus seems to us to be such as to make it of
absolutely unique value for human life and thought, our treatment

82

of the historical evidence concerning the life of Jesus will inevitably and rightly be different from what it would be, if we saw no such value in the Christian faith at all.

He goes on to say that while the believer must be prepared to admit the force of evidence which definitely shows some aspect of his belief to have been mistaken, he nevertheless is prepared to accept a reading of the evidence that the non-Christian critic cannot regard as adequately substantiated. And finally, in replying to the charge that he is allowing doctrinal prejudice to falsify history, Quick says:

The defence of the Christian's convictions about the historical origins of his faith will always rest mainly upon the principle that effects must have an adequate cause. And the judgement as to the adequacy of an alleged cause must always depend on a judgement as to the value of the given effect. Therefore our judgement as to the value of the Christian faith must necessarily affect our judgement as to the historical causes which are adequate to account for it.

That is why, in order to rebut the critics of incarnational Christology, it is necessary to stress the moral and religious value of the Incarnation as appreciated from within the Christian Church by a participating member, and, in the light of that, to consider the historical questions.[3]

As I say, this is a very delicate issue and the dangers of letting prejudice distort historical judgement are very great. In this connection, we do well to reflect on the monumental figure of Karl Barth. Barth was, in every way, a Church theologian. His *Church Dogmatics*[4] was written as an attempt to think through and present the faith of the Church in all its compelling intellectual and spiritual power. The task of showing, in such a magisterial and comprehensive way, the inner rationality of Christian doctrine, is an essential task for the Church theologian. But it has to be admitted that Barth is rather cavalier where the historical and critical study of the Bible is concerned. It may well be that it is his questionable rejection of apologetics that allows him to cut corners here.

The Incarnation

Barth is too ready to ignore the work of the biblical and historical critics on the grounds of their supposedly alien presuppositions. But Christian doctrinal theology, spelled out from within, cannot afford to remain so aloof from the critical questions.

There is undoubtedly a delicate question of balance here. The Church theologian will not wish to pursue doctrinal theology regardless of the genuine historical questions – but neither will he wish to study the history of Christian origins regardless of the faith of the Church of which he is a member. It is often said that it is philosophical presuppositions that introduce distortions into liberal Protestant Christology. That may be true of some attempts to restate the meaning of Christian doctrine. But one does not have to work with an alien philosophical framework to misjudge the historical evidence. An inappropriate impartiality or presuppositionless objectivity may also fail to yield the right perspective on the events with which we are concerned.

Lessons may be learned here from the history of the Roman Catholic Church in the twentieth century. For the dangers of Church theology cutting loose from its historical moorings are illustrated by the history of the turn-of-the-century Catholic Modernist movement. That movement shows how a sense of the religious value of the Christian tradition can become free-floating, self-sustaining and thoroughly implausible, precisely by cutting loose from its historical basis. The weakness of the Roman Church in dealing with the Modernist movement lay in its arbitrary veto on biblical criticism. The Modernists were most plausible in their acceptance of biblical criticism, least plausible in their sense of the tradition as religiously self-sustaining irrespective of its historical basis. The magisterium, in reaction, was most plausible in its insistence that doctrine must remain rooted in the facts, least plausible in trying to secure those facts by biblical fundamentalism. The lesson is that a proper doctrinal sensibility must be combined with a proper historical critical sensibility. The suggestion adumbrated here is that the former, with its recognition that doctrine is Church doctrine, provides the right context in which to exercise the latter. But maintaining the right balance is indeed no easy task.

Recent Roman Catholic theology has made great strides towards a proper balance. Belatedly, a sensitive and scholarly approach to biblical criticism and historical research into the origins of Christian doctrine has been combined with the systematic articulation of the meaning of the Catholic faith for modern man. One rightly expects the Roman Catholic theologians to be less susceptible to the dangers of allegedly context-free investigation of Christian origins and the development of doctrine. They are much more likely to be self-consciously Church theologians. But all is not well with Roman Catholic Christology. This state of affairs even merited an article in *Time Magazine*,[5] in which a number of Roman Catholic theologians were named for whom, it was alleged, 'Christ is not as divine as he used to be'. Pride of place was given to Hans Küng; but among others mentioned were the Dutch Jesuit, Piet Schoonenberg, the French Dominican, Jacques Pohier, the Spaniard, José-Ramon Guerrero, director of catechetics at Madrid's Pastoral Institute, and Jon Sobrino of El Salvador, author of the best-known Latin American Liberation Theology Christology. And, of course, the Schillebeeckx affair has received widespread publicity.

It has already been remarked that Roman Catholic theologians are unlikely to try to study Christian origins regardless of the context of the faith of the Church. What we do find, however, is a willingness to rethink that faith radically in the light of what they think can make sense to modern man. It is in this connection that men like Küng and Schillebeeckx are accused of repeating all the errors of liberal Protestantism in bringing alien presuppositions to bear upon the task of historical and doctrinal reconstruction – a charge levelled against them by Barthians such as T. F. Torrance,[6] as well as by the Congregation of the Faith in Rome. But is this charge justified? We must endeavour to be fair to the intentions of these Roman Catholic theologians. They are, after all, Church theologians, thinking through the doctrines of the faith on the basis of participation in her tradition and liturgy – and they are now able to embrace the methods of biblical criticism and explore the historical basis of the faith much more sensitively and openly than before. Moreover the Roman Catholics lack the Barthian prejudice against apologetic, and are able now to use historical critical methods in order to lead people gently from the facts concerning Jesus right through to the faith of the Church. This surely is what both Küng and Schillebeeckx are trying to do. But have they succeeded in doing this, or have they succumbed to the errors of liberal Protestantism in letting purely secular presuppositions come to control their doctrinal reconstructions? It seems that Küng is indeed open to criticism on this score, but that Schillebeeckx has been misunderstood and, at least on the central issues, unfairly criticised.

Something will be said in the second part of this paper about the way in which Küng and Schillebeeckx have been treated by the Vatican. Our concern here is the substantial issue of their understanding of Christian doctrine. It is a great pity, though perhaps inevitable, that Vatican criticism of Küng concentrated on his provocative work on infallibility. Küng's treatment of this topic in fact has much to be said for it. He provides an extremely plausible account of indefectibility in the truth through fallible human media. Such a view enables the Christian theologian to insist that the Church in which the Spirit of the risen Christ is encountered in prayer and sacrament cannot have been wholly mistaken in its christological and trinitarian doctrines as they have been developed and taught down the ages – even though any one formulation or expression of those truths may well be fallible and must be subject to critical investigation. Indeed such an account of indefectibility might well provide a way out of the impasse that exists between Anglicans and Roman Catholics over the infallibility dogma. This seemed to have been the opinion of the Anglican–Roman Catholic International Commission in its third report.[7] Moreover, as was ironically pointed out by a Roman Catholic theologian in Rome, Pope John Paul II's pastoral letter to the German bishops, congratulating them on the way in which they had dealt with Küng, went on to spell out and defend the infallibility dogma in terms not all that different from Küng's own statement of indefectibility. It is a great pity therefore that infallibility was made the main bone of contention for the Vatican, though, as I say, it was probably inevitable, given the provocative way in which Küng wrote about infallibility. However, the Vatican also showed itself to be suspicious of Küng's Christology, and here they were on stronger ground. Küng's book, *On Being a Christian*,[8] is certainly a most impressive work. No less a person than Albino Luciani, when he was Archbishop of Venice, wrote to Küng congratulating him on it. In many ways it carries out the task of apologetics along the lines advocated earlier in this chapter. With great historical sensitivity and with great pastoral concern for modern men and women in the full context of their self-understanding and aspirations, Küng seeks to recover the real Christ and his significance for individuals, for the Church and for the world. But a careful reading of pages 436–50 of *On Being a Christian* does not inspire confidence in Küng's faithfulness to the Church's tradition on the central question whether, in the end of the day, it can continue to be taught that Christ comes to us from the side of God and that that thoroughly human life, so well delineated in Küng's book, is still to be confessed to be the human face of *God*. It can hardly be denied that, where Küng is concerned, there are traces of the kind of

87

christological reductionism which seeks to replace the ontology implied in the classical doctrine of Christ by functional categories; what matters is what God is doing in and through the man Jesus; and that, as pointed out above, entails the loss of elements essential to the faith.

With Schillebeeckx the situation is different. Here, the Vatican did single out his Christology for attack, or, more properly, for investigation; but in Schillebeeckx's case they failed to do justice to or even to understand his intention in the first volume of his trilogy – the book *Jesus, an Experiment in Christology*,[9] which was the only work that the experts of the Congregation of the Faith had before them at the time. Schillebeeckx's intention in that book was deliberately to restrict himself to historical enquiry (though explicitly as a Church theologian, himself committed to the Church's doctrine, and so, on the view defended here, getting the perspective right for judging the historical evidence), and to trace the continuity from the man Jesus, his teaching, passion, death and resurrection, through the impact made upon the early Church, to the Church's interpretation of who this man Jesus is.

This interpretation is borne out by Schillebeeckx's second volume, *Christ*,[10] and by his *Interim Report*,[11] which is perhaps the most accessible introduction to Schillebeeckx's Christology. It is possible, therefore, to make a more positive assessment of Schillebeeckx's Christology than of Küng's. Both, it seems, are trying to do the same thing – to get back to the historical events that lie at the origin of the Church's faith, to show what is special about these origins, and at the same time to show the continuity between them and the faith of the creeds. But where the doctrine of the Incarnation is concerned, Schillebeeckx undoubtedly inspires more confidence than does Küng. It may be added that it does Schillebeeckx's cause no good at all to try to defend precisely the interpretation which the Vatican put upon him, as does

Peter Hebblethwaite in *The New Inquisition?*.[12] It seems, rather, that the Vatican simply misunderstood Schillebeeckx's intention.

A careful comparison of pages 669–70 of Schillebeeckx's *Jesus* with the passage from Küng referred to above should serve to bring out the difference between the two theologians. Both combine serious historical–critical study of the origins of Christianity with dogmatic–apologetic reflection on the Church's teaching. In both cases their aim, as self-consciously Church theologians, is faithfully to answer the questions: who is this Jesus, and what does he mean for us today? If Schillebeeckx is to be preferred to Küng on the question of fundamental Christology, it is because the latter, unlike the former, has allowed himself, despite his Catholic perspective, to become too influenced by liberal Protestantism in his assessment of how Church doctrine can be meaningfully interpreted for today.

In the second part of this chapter, I turn to the question of what the Church's attitude should be to the prevalence of doctrinal heterodoxy among some of the Church's theologians and also to the question of what the Church should do about it. It is well known that the Roman Catholic Church exercises stricter discipline on these matters than does the Church of England. Moreover the story of the Roman Catholic Church's disciplinary procedures, even in the twentieth century, is not inspiring. This is not only a matter of the actual procedures being so heavy-handed and contrary to elementary human rights, but also of much very proper scholarly work tending to get suppressed along with the views that actually were heretical. Thus the harsh suppression of Catholic Modernism by Pius X in the first decade of this century involved not only the very proper condemnation of the doctrinal views of Loisy and Tyrrell, but also set Roman Catholic biblical scholarship back for more than two generations. And to return to the

Küng and Schillebeeckx affairs, it has to be admitted that Peter Hebblethwaite's *The New Inquisition?*, despite the theological weaknesses to which I have referred, tells a sorry tale of secretive procedures and highly improper treatment of the accused that no one would wish to see emulated in the other Churches. Moreover, as was argued in the first part of this paper, the Vatican seems to have taken perhaps justified measures against Küng for largely the wrong reasons, and to have begun unjustified proceedings against Schillebeeckx through misunderstanding his work.

Anglican policy in recent years, by contrast, has apparently been to take no action. It is well known that the former archbishop, Michael Ramsey, now regrets the public rebuke which he gave the late John Robinson at the time of the publication of *Honest to God*,[13] a work which now seems relatively conservative.

This question of Church discipline of theologians over doctrinal matters may be illuminated by a concrete and specific example from the German Evangelical Church. The case is that of Professor Rudolf Bultmann.[14] In 1947 a certain Pastor Bruns in Marburg wrote to his Landesbischof, the Lutheran Bishop Wurm, raising a matter that had clearly become very painful to him. He had recently heard a public lecture by Bultmann, in which the Professor had used such formulae as 'the legend of the empty tomb', which had greatly disturbed him. He had written to Bultmann, and received a courteous reply, but one in which Bultmann had asked, 'Is it unknown to you that there are hardly any scholarly theologians who do not hold the story of the empty tomb to be a legend?'. Pastor Bruns found this very shocking. He did not actually believe Bultmann's remarks about most theologians, and he suggested that the Church should appoint a second – and more conservative – New Testament theologian to a chair in Marburg to counteract the teaching of Bultmann. He also suggested that the Church should set up more seminaries of its own, where sound teaching could be ensured. (These suggestions reflect the fact that in Germany the training of ordinands is for the most part entrusted much more to theological Faculties in the universities than it is in England, and that the Church has some direct responsibility in the appointment of University Professors, as was also true of Küng's appointment in Tübingen.)

Landesbischof Wurm took Pastor Bruns' letter very seriously indeed and proceeded to write to Karl Barth to ask his advice on how the matter should be handled. The details of Wurm's letter, which shows a considerable grasp of Bultmann's position against its theological background, need not detain us. It is worth mentioning, however, that Wurm had the courtesy to send a copy of his letter to Bultmann himself – an elementary courtesy apparently unknown to the Vatican.

Barth replied with a long letter, and he too sent a copy to Bultmann. He began by sketching the history of Bultmann's theology from the early 1920s on, stressing that Bultmann had always remained faithful to the fundamental aim and intention of confronting the human subject with God's self-revelation. But, said Barth, Bultmann increasingly came to feel that this could only be done on the basis of a particular philosophical anthropology that provided a 'pre-understanding' of man's situation and predicament. He combined this, on Barth's view, with an unequalled critical facility in New Testament scholarship; moreover he never wavered from the right side in the Church struggle against Hitler. Nevertheless Barth held that Bultmann's reliance on existentialist philosophy represented a fundamental mistake, and a presupposition of method that led him into great errors in Christology – not just over the resurrection, but over the incarnation and soteriology as well. Indeed, said Barth, 'I do not refrain from saying that I am bound to hold these views to be "heretical", that is, incompatible with the Church's confession of faith.' But this is the inevitable consequence, he continued, of operating on those presuppositions. And then, with a characteristically Barthian touch, he added that it was one of Bultmann's greatest services to theology, to carry the argument through so faithfully and thoroughly that we see where it leads.

Next, Barth turned to Pastor Bruns' specific complaints and endeavoured to show how unsatisfactory it would be for the Church to cross swords with Bultmann on those grounds. He pointed out that a phrase like 'the legend of the empty tomb' could be given a perfectly acceptable meaning. The literary genre 'legend' is not necessarily a negative thing. (Similar points are rightly made today about the term 'myth'.) On any theologically informed view, the Resurrection could not easily be classified along with ordinary historical facts. Bruns' response was quite the wrong way to react to Bultmann. Pastor Bruns, said Barth, appeared to have no idea of the nature and magnitude of the problem raised by Bultmann's work, which concerned the Church's whole Christology and raised questions of fundamental theological method. An ill-informed attack on Bultmann would only be counter-productive. For the Church to dispute with him at that level would do far more harm than good. (Again, one is reminded of the misunderstandings involved in the Vatican's attack on Schillebeeckx and how damaging to the Church itself that has been.) Barth said categorically that the harm done by such proceedings against Bultmann would be far greater than that done by Bultmann's writings and teaching, whose positive aim and intention, despite his 'heresies', should always be remembered. The German Church was not going to come to grief just because that sharp critic, himself the object of so much theological criticism, existed there in Marburg.

Barth then made a most important point. He reminded the Bishop that, when the Confessing Church in 1933–4 did have to make a stand against the German Christians who had capitulated to Hitler's racist views, the attack was launched not against particular remarks or deeds of particular German Christians but against the fundamental theological errors of that whole generation. Similarly now, the Church should either go to the root of the trouble and deal with that, or leave well alone. Barth had no time at all for Bruns' request for more seminaries or a more orthodox second Professor in Marburg.

Barth concluded his letter by saying that there would be no need to worry about Bultmann if the Church, in its preaching and church order, its church politics and its whole relation to state and society, were really bearing witness to the risen Christ. A second more orthodox Professor in Marburg would not rescue the Church from Bultmann, nor would disciplinary procedures against Bultmann. The only thing that would really confute Bultmann would be a Church living in the power of the risen One. Certainly Bultman should be answered, Barth continued, but that could be left to the theologians, who were already engaging with him in the only appropriate way – that of scholarly debate. Barth admitted that a situation might arise where the Church would have authoritatively to condemn a certain line of teaching, just as the Confessing Church had to do in the case of the German Christians – but that would be a matter of producing something like the Barmen Declaration, not of attacking named individuals. In fact Barth did not think this was called for in the case of Bultmann's teaching. All that was required was that the Church should faithfully be the Church. That would confute Bultmann far more successfully than any measures taken against him.

This example from an earlier dispute over alleged heretical teaching by a theologian does not enable us to solve all our present problems in face of the advocacy of non-incarnational Christology and non-trinitarian theology by certain theologians in our midst. But it may suggest some guidelines – that disciplinary measures against individuals are unlikely to be the best way forward, that theological error is best answered by better theology, and that the Church's answer must always be that of faithful witness in word and deed to the risen Christ. A Church that is resolutely the Church of Christ can tolerate, indeed profit from, provocative critics in its midst, if only by way of seeing the truth more clearly by contrast with the error.

The Anglican Church, as Stephen Sykes has recently reminded us,[15] sets a great deal of store by its liturgical life and by the doctrine expressed in its services and ordinal. If non-incarnational and non-trinitarian theology began to be reflected in these, then there would indeed be cause for alarm. But there is no sign of that at present.

8

Christ today and tomorrow

In this chapter I want to examine the question whether the Church may one day, after all, come to endorse the views of the authors of *The Myth of God Incarnate*. At a conference in Lancaster in 1973 when John Hick put forward for the first time the views which he later developed, in the *Myth* book and elsewhere, about Jesus being one among a number of creative religious innovators who have enabled different streams of human history to grow in the knowledge of God, a conference member observed ruefully, 'I suppose in a hundred years time we shall all be saying that kind of thing.' I want to ask if that is true. It is likely or even possible that the Church's understanding of its faith might develop to the point where not only individual theologians but the Church itself – in its confessions and liturgies as well as in guidelines offered by bishops, teaching offices and so on – might come to endorse a non-incarnational Christology.

This question must be considered in the context of the whole problem of the development of Christian doctrine. It is, of course, a platitude to say that all religions change and develop. Whatever else they are, religions are human historical phenomena, and everything human and everything historical changes and develops. This is true of every human historical aspect of every religion – their beliefs, their practices, their institutions, their forms of liturgy. The reason why change and development constitute a problem for religions more than they do for other human historical phenomena is that religions for the most part understand themselves as not only historical phenomena but custodians and transmitters of divine truth. There is a strong and understandable tendency, especially in religions such as Christianity and Islam, which stress divine revelation, to deny that divine truth changes or develops. On the contrary, they think it is immutable. (Such religions vary in the extent to which they admit that human understanding of divine truth changes and develops.) These very general reflections introduce us to a basic distinction. It can best be expressed in the form of two questions: to what extent do the truth and realities to which Christianity points change and develop? (In the eyes of most Christians that is a question expecting the answer, not at all.) And, secondly, to what extent does the Church's understanding of and expression of those fundamental truths change and develop? (That is a question to which we have learned to expect the answer, a great deal, and necessarily so.) But one cannot make this distinction without raising three further questions. If changes and developments in understanding and expression do and must occur, might they not be for the worse rather than for the better; is there any control over the direction and extent of these changes and developments; and are there any valid criteria by which to distinguish good from bad changes and developments?

The whole 'Myth' debate shows what a central issue this is in modern theology. It is the central issue in the Church of England Doctrine Commission's report *Christian Believing*, which appeared in 1976.[1] That report was remarkable not only for the plurality of views it contained, but also for its endorsement of pluralism in ways of believing and in ways of understanding Christian faith as something here to stay. In particular there is explicit recognition of four very different approaches to the Christian creeds within the Church of England today: first, the view that the creeds are a norm of Christian belief, embodying the permanent truth of the

Gospel; secondly, the view that identifies itself with the general faith of the Church which expresses itself in those creeds, though it permits the questioning of individual clauses, such as that relating to the Virgin Birth; thirdly, the view that, though formed by the Church and its creeds, Christians' primary loyalty should be to the continuing Church of God as it testifies to the truth of God today; and fourthly, the view that the essence of faith lies in a life of discipleship rather than in credal affirmations. Of particular interest is the third of these approaches – the one which holds that Christians' primary loyalty is to the continuing Church of God as it tries to express the truth of God today, because here we seem to get an explicit endorsement by a Church body of the possibility that Christian self-understanding may develop away from its historically and culturally conditioned roots into something very different from what came to expression in the Bible and the creeds.

Theologians will be very familiar with this approach. At a recent gathering it was insisted by a well-known theologian that one could not say in principle that the Church's self-understanding could *never* develop to the point where it endorsed the views of Don Cupitt in his book, *Taking Leave of God*.[2] Similarly, at an ecumenical conference in Cambridge, it was insisted that we could not tell in advance what are the limits to theology's struggle not only to understand but to modify the faith by which the Church sought to live. Admittedly, it was agreed in the discussion that there *were* limits: one could hardly end up affirming the very opposite of what had been the faith of Christians down the ages; but it was certainly held that no one could say in advance whether or not some radical though less drastic modification would be a legitimate development or not. The qualification gave little comfort. For views are advanced in Christian theology today which do not seem very far removed from the opposite of the Church's traditional faith. So further questions arise. Who is to judge these matters? Is each theologian a judge in his own cause? Or is the Church the arbiter of legitimate development? And what do we mean by the Church here – the bishops? – the magisterium? – the Doctrine Commission? – the General Synod? – the general consensus in the Church? The latter perhaps sounds most plausible; but may not the Church fall into error, as well as the theologians and the bishops?

These problems will be tackled here from three different angles. First, attention will be focused on the truths and realities to which Christianity claims to bear witness. In what sense are they either immutable or changing and developing? Then attention will be shifted to our understanding and expression of those truths, which, we are almost bound to admit, do change and develop – this is the question of the development of doctrine proper. Then, thirdly, we shall turn to the vexed questions of control and criteria.

The first question, then, is to what extent must it be held that divine truth is immutable, that is, *not* subject to change and development? Presumably most Christians would want to say that God is God or that God is who he is without variation or shadow of turning. Of course, process theologians and others would raise objections even at this basic starting-point. They would wish to question the idea that God is static and immutable. Rather, they would say, God exists in process, in becoming, in acting. Indeed most theologians would now affirm that, at least in his relation to the world, God is a God who acts, and that the story of God's dealings with his people constitutes an unfolding and indeed unfinished history. One does not have to be a process theologian to go even further than this and claim to discern behind the history of God's dealings with creation, the history of God's own being – the trinitarian history of God, as Jürgen Moltmann has called it.[3] There is no doubt that Christian theology as a whole has come to operate with a much more dynamic conception of God. The influence of Platonism is on the wane.

So our conception of divine immutability must be reformulated. There seem to be two elements in the idea of divine immutability, however, that Christian theists must retain. In the first place they will want to insist on the unchangeable nature of God's character as manifested in his acts – his steadfastness both in purpose and in action, his reliability and his trustworthiness. And in the second place they will want to insist on the fact that what God has done he has done. If he has provided a unique and normative revelation of himself in Jesus Christ, then that is what he has done. That fact stands fast, however we may change and develop in our comprehension of God's self-revealing act.

So God remains the same, yesterday, today and for ever in his character and purpose. And what he has done by acts of self-revealing love, he has done, and there is no changing those facts – if facts they are. It seems then that something is left of the notion of immutable divine reality and truth. God may exist in process and becoming and acting. There may indeed be a divine history – but this history constitutes in itself an immutable reality, in the sense that what God has done he has done, and the reality of God's unchanging character and trustworthiness, as manifested in the divine history, remains immutable as well. This means that divine truth remains immutable too – for, ultimately speaking, truth and reality are one. The unchanging realities of God's character and acts constitute unchanging truths to be apprehended as accurately as possible by our minds. They are of course already known in full by divine omniscience.

But there remains a problem. Once the move has been made from a static to a dynamic conception of God and the immutable truth acknowledged that God is a God who acts, it has to be admitted that the story of God's acts, in the nature of the case, is incomplete. We find ourselves in the middle of the story, not at the end. Creation is in process. The consummation of creation is yet to come. God's redemptive acts are not yet over; for men and women not only have been saved, but are being saved and will be saved, as commentators on St Paul remind us. The same holds true of revelation. Revelation has a history. It may have reached a climax in Jesus Christ, but it cannot be supposed that revelation comes to an abrupt stop with the resurrection and ascension of Christ. The divine Spirit, rather, is believed to continue to lead the disciples of Christ into all truth, and there is a sense in which the Church *waits* for God's glory to be revealed in the last day.

It is this factor – the unfinished and unconsummated nature of the story of God's acts – that makes some theologians (such as Gerald Downing)[4] wary of the use of the very idea of divine revelation, and makes others (such as Wolfhart Pannenberg)[5] emphasise the futurity of God in his final dealings with creation. Even so, the facts remain that God is who he is and that God has done what he has done, even if there are further things yet that he will do and even if the story is incomplete. The crucial question remains: *What* is it that God has (immutably) done? Whatever is done in the future, the past cannot be changed – although no doubt what is done in the future may change the significance of and people's attitude to what was done in the past.

The burden of this first section, then, is that, in so far as theology concentrates on the reality of God and of God's acts, there must be a sense in which there are immutable divine realities and truths – even if God's dealings with the world are dynamic and in process, and even if they are incomplete and only to be consummated in the future. Where Christology is concerned, the key question that arises from these considerations is whether it really is the case that God, in the person of his Son, became man in Jesus of Nazareth for the redemption of the world. Incarnational Christology holds that that was indeed the case and that that *fact* is one of the immutable realities to which the Church's doctrine bears witness.

We turn now to the second question – the question of human understanding and expression of these immutable divine realities and truths. The Church sums up its understanding of these matters in its doctrines. It would certainly not be easy to defend the view that Church doctrine is immutable. This is the point at which some change and development must surely be admitted.

The firm distinction drawn here between the immutable facts of who God is and what he has done on the one hand and the changing and developing understanding of those facts in Church doctrine on the other may elicit strong objections from the more philosophically inclined. After all, our only access to who God is and to what God has done is through human witness, human interpretation, understanding and expression. It is precisely the changing and developing doctrines which mediate the facts of the matter to us. There is no independent access to the facts which could enable us to check the adequacy of our understanding. Even our own experience of God is apprehended in the light of an inherited developing tradition and is subject, of course, to the limitations of our own powers of understanding and expression. This is a very general problem. It does not arise only in the case of our knowledge of God. In any sphere of knowledge, this realist emphasis on the facts being what they are and our understanding of the facts being limited and developing encounters the same difficulty. There is no independent access to any facts except through fallible and developing human understanding. The philosophy of science is constantly preoccupied with just this problem in respect of our knowledge of the physical world around us.

Notwithstanding these facts, it still helps to maintain the

distinction between the realities and actions themselves and our attempts to understand and express them. For one thing it helps to remind us that we are not inventing the world about us. In the case of knowledge of God, we are not inventing God and God's acts. We are discovering them, receiving them, responding to them. In the second place, it helps to remember that this matter of understanding and expression – in the case before us, this matter of doctrine – is a question of many millions of different people down the ages responding to and apprehending the same reality and acts of God. It is not our own private personal interpretation. It is a common task, and Christians must learn from each other and from the past. In the third place, to hold on to this distinction between immutable realities and changing understanding helps us to retain the idea of better and better approximation to the facts, better and better understanding of what God has done. There are good reasons therefore for refusing to abandon this basic realist approach just because there is no other access to the facts than fallible human witness and interpretation.

But why is there bound to be change and development in interpretation, understanding and doctrine? The reason is a very simple one: our modern sense of history has taught us to recognise the historically, culturally and socially conditioned nature of all human responses. We have come to recognise this where the Bible is concerned. It is almost impossible for a historically sensitive person to treat the Bible as itself God's self-revelation. It has to be understood as a human historically and culturally conditioned collection of witnesses to divine revelation. We have come to recognise this where the creeds are concerned. That there is a human story behind the formation of the creeds and that that story and the creeds themselves reflect not only particular situations but particular historically and culturally conditioned ways of looking at the world cannot be denied. So even if the

Christian mind continues to hold that the Bible and the creeds are pointing to and summing up men's apprehension of immutable divine realities and truths, we still have to recognise their historical limitations and the fact that we live in a different world with a different, though still limited and partial, apprehension of ourselves, the world and God. It is not even possible for us to *mean* what the writers of the Bible and the creeds meant just by saying what they said. We have to embark on the process of interpretation, in the light of our recognition both of their presuppositions and of our own, and struggle to express the truth of God and of God's acts for our own time. The history of the development of Christian doctrine is the story of generation after generation of Christians trying to do just that. The Protestant Churches have been grappling with this problem for nearly 200 years now. They have tended to call it the problem of hermeneutics. The Roman Catholic Church has tended to stick to the phrase 'the development of doctrine', but latterly it has become just as aware of the historical problem as the Protestants have been. For a time the Vatican tried to stem the tide – it suppressed the Catholic Modernist movement early in this century – but the problems could not be buried; they resurfaced to form the background to Vatican II, and they constitute one of the main themes in the writings of Roman Catholic theologians such as Rahner, Schillebeeckx, Küng and Lonergan.

There was, already, an intriguing example of this basic problem in the first Vatican Council of 1870, even though that Council was part of the doomed effort to stem the tide. Vatican I affirmed that the meaning of Church dogma was immutable, but allowed that its form and expression changed. That was to introduce a thoroughly realist sense of 'meaning'. The meaning of the doctrines of the Church was there equated with their reference, with the realities themselves. What the doctrines really mean or intend to express is what God has done. Reality, truth and meaning all coalesce. They

103

are what the doctrines are about. But then the basic problem only reappears as the distinction between what the doctrines really mean and what people, including the bishops and the theologians, understand by them in each successive age. In this terminology the meaning remains the same, our expression of this meaning changes and develops.

Current christological disputes illustrate this problem well. One way of characterising *The Myth of God Incarnate* debate would be to see it as concerned with the question whether the Church's teachings about the person of Christ are changing and developing ways of interpreting the *fact* that God, in one of the centres of his being, took human nature into himself and became man in Jesus of Nazareth, or whether the notion of God made man is just one, time-conditioned and now outmoded, way of expressing the significance of Jesus for the believer. The authors of *The Myth* maintain that talk of incarnation is part of the changing husk, and that what matters – the kernel – is the sense of God that Jesus mediates to Christians, while their opponents maintain that it is the changing terminology and concepts of Church doctrine that are the husk, and the reality – God's becoming man – is the kernel. This is not at all an easy dispute to resolve. But clearly, if the authors of *The Myth* are right, then the Church may find its doctrine developing in a non-incarnational direction. If their opponents are right, it will not; for what God has done stands fast, even if the Church's understanding of it changes.

How slippery a slope the authors of *The Myth* are on may be gathered from one of their number, Don Cupitt's, subsequent writing on the doctrine of God. The question now becomes whether the Church's changing and developing doctrine of God is the human response to the infinite source of all there is making himself known to us as the God of love – or whether God-talk as such is part of the changing and developing expression of an unconditional religious conviction of the claims of disinterestedness and spirituality.

It would certainly be much easier if we could block this whole process at the start and say that the Bible or the dogmas of the Church are themselves God's immutable self-revelation for all time, that they escape the relativities of historical and cultural conditioning. But few serious theologians today would be able to accept that kind of 'pure datum' theory. Even if it is agreed that revelation is never unmediated, but that God's acts and God's revelation have to be discerned in and through all-too-human vehicles or media and that the reception of revelation is also mediated, there still remains a difference between those who think that the characteristic doctrines of Christianity down the ages – Trinity, Incarnation, Redemption, Resurrection, Kingdom – though partial and conditioned in their formulation, remain true and capable of reformulation in each successive age, and those who think that the Church's self-understanding may develop or evolve into completely new forms, unpredictable, and only connected with past forms in the historical sense that new generations of Christians are, simply as a matter of fact, nourished by the faith which they find themselves led to modify beyond recognition.

The third main question is whether there is any control or criterion whereby false, inappropriate or distorting developments may be detected and prevented, and a stable future for Christian doctrine predicted. There is no easy answer to this question. It seems that, short of implausible claims to infallibility, the Church can only proceed in the *faith* that, if Christianity is indeed the response to the being and acts of God, then in the end truth will out and erroneous and inappropriate expressions of Christian faith will sooner or later be detected and corrected. In other words, Christianity carries within itself an assumption of the indefectibility of God's truth – even if that truth is always transmitted by fallible, all-too-human vehicles. This built-up assumption makes it implausible to suppose that the Church might endorse the 'Myth' view in the future.

A careful examination of Christianity, its background in Judaism, its emergence on the basis of the events concerning Jesus, and its history, both in the initial formative centuries and ever since, reveals a religion that cannot be thought of as no more than a set of spiritual experiences. Rather its defining characteristic is its claim to witness to God's acts for man's redemption. Such a belief entails that if God has indeed acted in history for man's salvation – however mediated those acts were, through a people and through a particular man and through the response of other people to that man – then those acts and events in the past are bound to exercise constraint and control over later interpretations. The history of the development of doctrine bears this out. Historical Christianity cannot be construed as a continuously evolving and expanding stream of spiritual experience interpreted in ever new ways. The history of the Church constitutes rather an ebb and flow of modification and reformation – renewed attempts to recover the real meaning of the crucial determining events. This is to refer not only to the Protestant Reformation of the sixteenth century, but to numerous other reformation movements, including dialectical theology and Vatican II in our own time. Conversely, it may be pointed out that suggestions like those of the authors of *The Myth* are no new phenomenon. These views have been tried out before and no doubt will be tried out again – but each time they are found wanting. They do not do justice to the crucial events which gave birth to Christianity, and so there is a reaction and a recovery of the first Gospel, not in the form in which it was first preached; it must indeed be translated and expressed in new cultural and historical contexts. But the movement is always back and then forward, not just on and on and on, moving further and further away from its origins.

The ideas behind the doctrine of indefectibility are, therefore: first that truth and reality are bound in the end to prevail, and second that, if God has acted decisively in the past, then that past history, however hard to recapture, is bound, ever and again, to constitute a check and a control on our understanding and expression of divine truth.

At this point, the function of the Bible must be considered. Recognition of the human, culturally and socially conditioned, nature of the Old and New Testament writings does not prevent the Church from holding that the most immediate human witness to the revelatory events will always constitute a check and control on the development of doctrine. In many ways the world of the Bible is a strange world, and in any case it has to be admitted that the New Testament contains only the raw material of Christian doctrine. But if God acted in a special and decisive way in that strange world, and if, for all its strangeness, the Church today stands within a continuous line of participation in the effects of that special action, then it cannot cut itself off from those events and from their first witnesses and still regard itself as the Christian Church. Moreover the Bible is there. It is a fact and no conceivable development of Christian doctrine could ignore it or write it off. It certainly needs interpreting, but unless the Church's interpretations commend themselves as interpretations of those events and that collection of first witnesses, they are unlikely to carry conviction for long.

The New Testament, as has just been pointed out, provides only the raw material for Christian doctrine; and indeed the process of hammering out the meaning of the Christ-event into creeds and confessions took a long period of time. It helps, of course, if continuity can be shown between the New Testament witness and the credal doctrines of the Trinity and the Incarnation. It is in this connection that C. F. D. Moule, in his *The Origin of Christology*,[6] has urged the 'development' model as opposed to the 'evolution' model. His argument is that we can see in the credal doctrines the unfolding and making explicit of something already implicit in the New Testament. If, by contrast, the doctrines represent completely new growths, new species in a process of evolution, they may well be treated with suspicion, whether they emerge in the fifth century or the nineteenth or the twentieth.

But how normative should creeds and confessions be? Certainly in each age the Church will wish to sum up its understanding of Christian faith in its own context and in relation to its dominant concerns; but it is hard to recognise the Christian Church as maintaining its identity if it writes off or modifies beyond recognition the decisions of broadly based and carefully considered statements of belief by earlier generations of Christians. This is especially true of the early creeds when the characteristic shape of Christian doctrine was hammered out for the first time. The reason why special weight is attached to the early creeds is the same as the reason why special weight is attached to the Bible, namely that Christianity claims to be a response to God's acts in history and a structure built on those foundation events. On the other hand, no creed or council or confession escapes the relativities of history. No creed can itself be treated as immutable divine revelation. Hence the need to show the continuity between the foundation events and the Bible and the creeds. Hence the need to *show* the positive ability of the historic creeds to transmit and illuminate Christian faith, notwithstanding their embeddedness in a particular historical context.

So the control of the foundational events over present developing understanding of Christian faith can be seen to be mediated by the first scriptural witnesses, then by the first considered credal summaries, and then by Church tradition down the ages. And the very fact that Christianity claims to be based on certain acts of God in the past requires us to show both the continuity between scripture and tradition and the ability of tradition to transmit and illuminate Christian faith through successive, changing, indeed radically new, historical and cultural contexts.

The tradition is not a new source of revelation. Christianity has always maintained the fundamental distinction between immutable divine realities and acts and changing human comprehension of what God has done. This does not mean that God is held to have stopped acting with the resurrection and ascension of Jesus. Both Bible and tradition speak of the acts of God by his Spirit in every age, leading Christians into all truth. But for Christian faith, it is the truth of *Christ* that the Spirit makes plain and that enables the Church to apply and to live out in every new age and in every new historical and social context. In other words, it is a characteristic feature of the shape of Christianity that Christian understanding down the ages is determined and controlled by what God did in Christ. It is a sense of this characteristic shape of Christianity, worked out in the doctrines of Incarnation, Redemption and Trinity, that resists the suggestion that Christian faith might develop and change and modify itself to the point where those characteristic central doctrines are tacitly dropped or translated out of all recognition.

But who is to decide these matters? If it is the faith of the Church that is at issue, then it seems that any doctrinal development must, in the end, by submitted to the Church for recognition and endorsement. But what do we mean by the Church here? Certainly the bishops and pastors have a responsibility in this connection, but it is doubtful if these problems of continuity and legitimate development can be settled by the setting up of a doctrinal watchdog committee, such as the Congregation of the Faith in Rome. There is no guarantee that such bodies get things right. Nor can responsibility for these decisions be handed over to theologians. Theologians must be free to explore and to make suggestions for new understanding of the faith, but the Church will not receive their suggestions if the new understanding cannot be

109

related positively to what has gone before, and if the proposed development cannot be lived out and prayed out by Christians in the actual practice and worship of Christianity. Least of all does it make sense to suppose that, of all religions, Christianity can let go its historical origins and concede that for two thousand years it has been in fundamental error about its faith.

The suggestion adumbrated here, then, is that while there are no knock-down authorities any more than there are any knock-down criteria, the truth of God will continue to prevail in the life and worship as in the thought and reflection of the Church at large in every age. This is again to affirm belief not in infallibility, but in indefectibility, despite change and experiment and despite all errors and distortions. It follows that the Church should tolerate deviant theologians, since their very errors and mistakes show up the truth of the matter from another angle, if only by contrast. Christians can learn from *The Myth of God Incarnate*, even if it is very much in error and quite incapable of determining the Church's Christology in the future.

Two further topics may be mentioned in conclusion: other religions and ethics.

This chapter has concentrated on the development of Christian doctrine from the standpoint of Church theology. But one of the relatively new features of our contemporary religious situation which is bound to lead to some development in Christian understanding is the increasingly pluralist character of modern societies and the necessarily global nature of our religious concern. We are much more aware of other religions and we have to reckon with the facts and significance of other religions much more in Christian theology today. Recognition of the culturally and historically conditioned nature of all human responses to divine acts and divine revelation can help here to encourage a much more positive attitude to other religions. It frees the Christian theologian to look for what God has done and is doing in and through other faiths and it prevents him from absolutising his own Christian understanding. On this basis he can learn from other faiths and reinterpret the Christ-event in the light of the whole history of religions. He can expect to find both common ground and mutual constructive criticism in inter-faith dialogue. What he cannot do, of course, is assume or concede, as John Hick appears to do,[7] that God has acted equally in and through every major world faith. For specifically Christian faith is committed to the belief that the Christ-event represents a decisive breakthrough in the history of religions, as Paul Tillich called it.[8]

This chapter has concentrated on the development of *doctrine*. But equally Christian *practice* in new contexts and new situations is bound to change and develop as well. We notice this especially in respect of Christian social ethics. Modern political theology is often criticised as being something quite different from the ethical teaching of Jesus and of St Paul. But, as with doctrine, Christians today have to ask themselves whether or not these new developments in Christian social ethics do not bring out something implicit in the Christ-event that has to be unfolded in face of the demands and challenges of contemporary life. Again it is necessary to show the continuities and the basis in the Christian revelation for these developments. The Church will not be happy with those forms of liberation theology which glorify violence in a way quite contrary to Jesus' own way of the Cross. But many liberation theologians, such as Archbishop Helda Camara of Brazil, are pacifists, and their radicalism can quite plausibly be represented as an authentic development and not an entirely new species of Christian life.

9

The doctrine of the Incarnation in the thought of Austin Farrer

Austin Farrer was very much a rational theologian. In two senses was this so. First, the subject-matter of his most weighty books was rational theology, chiefly the grounds for theistic belief, but also the theology of nature and of freedom. He wrote much on God, providence and evil, but little on the doctrines of the Incarnation and the Trinity. Secondly, where he did treat of more doctrinal topics, his interest was always in the intelligibility and rationality of Christian belief. Even in his sermons and devotional writings, informed by catholic piety as they were, his philosophical mind is never in abeyance, and the clear and vivid statement of the sense of Christian doctrine was one of the preacher's chief aims.

To discover Farrer's views on Incarnation, then, we need to comb his writings, including the sermons, for incidental references and occasional paragraphs. There are, in the four published collections,[1] one or two sermons specifically on the Incarnation, but apart from these, the only more extended pieces on that doctrine are an article entitled 'Very God and Very Man', apparently written in the early fifties, and now published in *Interpretation and Belief*,[2] and chapter 3 of *Saving Belief*.[3]

In respect of doctrinal theology Austin Farrer can be described as an original and penetrating expositor of traditional Christian belief. He was orthodox rather than liberal, but he was not afraid to reject less central parts of the Christian

112

tradition, such as literal belief in the devil.[4] But there is no
evidence, where the doctrine of the Incarnation is concerned,
that Farrer was ever tempted to question the central belief of
catholic Christendom, that, in Jesus Christ, we have to do
with one who was and is 'very God and very Man'. He did,
however, want to understand and explicate that doctrine.

There is an interesting difference between Farrer's exten-
sive treatment of theistic metaphysics and his relatively
minimal treatment of the doctrine of Christ. Both are examined for their inner rationality and sense, but the former is
also justified in a way in which the latter is not. Indeed, in
'Very God and Very Man', Farrer disarmingly says: 'Look
here: the longer I go on trying to tell you about this, the more
I become convinced that the job that really wants doing is to
expound the formula rather than to justify it; or, anyhow,
that the justification required is identical with exposition.'[5]
This actually, and perhaps surprisingly, pinpoints the merits
of Farrer on Incarnation. When we see so clearly what the
doctrine means we come to appreciate its significance and
force, and to recognise how far from the mark are certain
modern liberal caricatures, such as those so easily knocked
down by the authors of *The Myth of God Incarnate*.

Let us look, then, at the salient features of the doctrine of
the Incarnation as expounded by Farrer in the course of his
writings. The first point to note is Farrer's stress on the contingency of the Incarnation. Rational theology cannot say *a
priori* whether or how God acts by providence or grace. 'We
cannot deduce the form of God's personal dealing with us
from the mere notion of a supreme personal Being.'[6] This
point had already been made forcefully in the closing
paragraph of *Finite and Infinite*:

As I wrote this, the German armies were occupying Paris, after a
campaign prodigal of blood and human distress. Rational theology
will not tell us whether this has or has not been an unqualified and
irretrievable disaster to mankind and especially to the men who

died. It is another matter if we believe that God Incarnate also died, and rose from the dead.[7]

The actual manner of God's personal dealings with us, then, is learned from revelation, and, as Farrer says in *The Glass of Vision*, 'the primary revelation is Jesus Christ himself'.[8] This comes out most clearly when Farrer speculates, in *Saving Belief*, on the question whether Christ would have come even if men had not sinned. 'Surely', he says, 'he would still have come . . . to transform human hope and to bring men into a more privileged association with their Creator than they could otherwise enjoy. For it is by the descent of God into man that the life of God takes on a form with which we have direct sympathy and personal union.'[9] Similarly, in 'Very God and Very Man', Farrer writes of 'Godhead dealing so humanely with us as to come in actual human being'.[10] The stress, then, is on the utterly gracious and personal nature of God's dealings with us through incarnation – the primary purpose of that incarnation being the making possible for us of genuinely personal union with God. 'The Gospel', writes Farrer in *A Science of God?*, 'presents to us . . . a God so personal, so particular and so present, that he collects his whole purpose for the world into one speaking action, by the entry of the divine life into the created sphere in the body and person of a man.'[11] The moral necessity of the Incarnation, which we come to recognise when we appreciate the personal knowledge of God which the Incarnation makes possible, was baldly expressed by Farrer in a sermon (in *A Celebration of Faith*): 'Unless God has gathered himself out of his immensity and come to me as man, I do not even know that he is God.'[12]

So the Incarnation is not contingent upon human sin. Nevertheless men are sinners and in fact the Incarnation is the means of salvation prior to personal union with God. 'What, then, did God do for his people's redemption?' asks Farrer in *Saving Belief*. 'He came amongst them, bringing his

kingdom, and he let events take their human course. He set
the divine life in human neighbourhood. Men discovered it in
struggling with it and were captured by it in crucifying it.'[13]
But the ultimate purpose of the Incarnation is, as I say, our
personal union with God. As Farrer puts it in *A Science of
God?*,

> To realise a union with our Creator we need not scale heaven or
> strip the veil from ultimate mystery; for God descends into his
> creature and acts humanly in mankind. He has made it our calling
> that we should have fellowship with himself; and so now by faith,
> but in heaven by sight, we are to look into the countenance divinely
> human and humanly divine of Christ the Lord.[14]

So far, we have noted the contingency of the Incarnation
and yet its inner moral necessity, given the nature of divine
personality and grace actually revealed in Christ. We must
now explore further what precisely Farrer understood by the
Incarnation. Already we have seen that he takes it to involve
God's own descent into man, by which God's personality and
love are revealed in action and suffering. So there is in Christ
coincidence of deity and manhood. In *The Glass of Vision*, Farrer writes: 'The Person of Christ, in the belief of Catholic
Christendom, is . . . the height of supernaturality; for in it the
first and second causes are personally united, the finite and infinite centres in some manner coincide; manhood is so taken
into God, that the human life of Jesus is exercised from the
centre of deity.'[15] Similarly we are encouraged in 'Very God
and Very Man' to think of 'human existence so rooted and
grounded in God's will and action as to be the personal life
of God himself, under the self-imposed conditions of a particular human destiny'.[16]

Three aspects of this doctrine need to be stressed if we are
to avoid misunderstanding. In the first place, it is the fact of
incarnation that shows both the personal nature of God and
the ultimate compatibility of God and man. In a sermon on
'Incarnation', to be found in *The Brink of Mystery*, Farrer

points out that the admittedly paradoxical notion of deity living out the life of a freelance rabbi is not the sheer nonsense of the supposition that God might have become incarnate in an unreasoning beast. 'Deity is reasonable mind, and cannot express himself personally through anything else; not, therefore, through an unreasoning creature.'[17] (There is scope here for reflection on the difference between this Christian concept of God and the Hindu belief in Vishnu, who takes animal as well as human form.) 'By contrast', Farrer goes on, 'the incarnation of God in a man makes sense: finite mind or person becomes the vehicle of infinite mind, infinite person.' Earlier, in the 'Revelation' essay in *Faith and Logic*, Farrer had argued that *Christian* theology must base its doctrine of divine personality on the possibility of incarnation rather than vice versa:

God must be in such sense a personal agent that he can be said voluntarily to adopt and really to use the human forms of life and action. A Christian who admits difficulties about incarnation from the divine side stands his theology up on its head. What positive knowledge has he of the divine personality which could exclude incarnation? On the contrary the divine personality is for him defined by incarnation; self-defined, indeed, and therefore revealed.[18]

Secondly, it is important to note that Farrer in no sense plays down the mystery of God. The mystery and the paradox remain, precisely in God's revelation through incarnation. 'Christ's person', he writes in *The Glass of Vision*, 'defeats our intellect, as deity defeats it, and for the same reason; for deity is in it.'[19] Interestingly, in a sermon to be found in *A Celebration of Faith*, Farrer argues that it is the reverse of the truth to suppose that the doctrine of the Incarnation involves an anthropomorphic view of God. On the contrary, 'it was the growing perception of God's immeasurable transcendence which provided the climate for his saving Incarnation'.[20] Primitive stories of God, Farrer avers, were so anthropomorphic that they did not need this self-humanising of God.

This is the point at which we must mention, in the third place, the trinitarian doctrine which Farrer emphasises so strongly in his expositions of the Incarnation, and which so far I have kept in the background. Farrer's trinitarian theology is developed most fully (though still not very fully) in the chapter entitled 'Law and Spirit' in *Saving Belief*, where he says boldly, 'the revealed parable of the Godhead is a story about two characters, Father and Son'.[21] This rather crude binitarian language is heavily qualified in the sequel in ways which would take us too far into the doctrine of the Spirit for present purposes, but it is important to bring out the fact that throughout his writings Farrer insists on the relational nature of God and on the fact that it is not deity *simpliciter* that became incarnate, but divine Sonship. The point is made in 'Very God and Very Man', where it forms part of a rather curious imaginary dialogue between a missionary in Africa and a native boy: 'It is not just Godhead that becomes incarnate, it is Godhead in the special form or person of Sonship. Divine Son becomes incarnate; and since Divine Son draws his whole person and being from the divine fatherhood anyhow quite apart from his incarnation, when he becomes incarnate he does not cease to do so.'[22] The eternal Sonship was similarly emphasised in *Lord, I Believe*: 'He is the Son of God, and his Sonship is simple and unalloyed derivation . . . The Son of God is the Word of the Father and more alive than any utterance because he comes new every moment out of the heart of God.'[23] The same point recurs often in the sermons, namely that Jesus' constant reference away from himself to the Father who sent him is the incarnate form of the eternal derivedness of the Son from the Father in the Blessed Trinity. The most emphatic example comes in the sermon on 'Incarnation' already quoted from *The Brink of Mystery*:

We cannot understand Jesus as simply the God-who-was-man. We have left out an essential factor, the sonship. Jesus is not simply God manifest as man, he is the divine Son coming in manhood.

117

What was expressed in human terms here below was not bare deity; it was divine sonship. God cannot live an identically godlike life in eternity and in a human story. But the divine Son can make an identical response to his Father, whether in the love of the blessed Trinity, or in the fulfilment of an earthly ministry. All the conditions of action are different on the two levels; the filial response is one. Above, the response is a co-operation in sovereignty and an interchange of eternal joys. Then the Son gives back to the Father all that the Father is. Below, in the incarnate life, the appropriate response is an obedience to inspiration, a waiting for direction, an acceptance of suffering, a rectitude of choice, a resistance to temptation, a willingness to die. For such things are the stuff of our existence and it was in this very stuff that Christ worked out the theme of heavenly sonship, proving himself on earth the very thing he was in heaven; that is, a continuous perfect act of filial love.[24]

I have given this long quotation in full, since we shall doubtless want to ask ourselves whether Farrer's insistence on this point is entirely justified. He was quite right, of course, to point out that the relation of Jesus to the Father reflects an inner-trinitarian relation, and that it only makes sense to think of Jesus as the incarnation of one of the poles or modes of the eternally relational deity. No doubt, too, that relation was bound, as far as the man Jesus was concerned, to express itself in terms of mission and dependence – a constant reference back to the fount and source of his life in God. But to see this as reflecting eternal derivedness or filiation in the Trinity is perhaps to go too far. One recalls the firm rejection by Leonard Hodgson of such residual subordinationism in his excellent book *The Doctrine of the Trinity*,[25] and I find it interesting to note that in fact, when Farrer tries to spell the matter out in the sermon on 'Incarnation', he finds himself speaking of the Father–Son relation 'above' in the Blessed Trinity as consisting in 'a co-operation in sovereignty and an interchange of eternal joys'.[26] Farrer himself has dropped the subordinationist language there. Be that as it may, it is quite clear that, to make sense of the Incarnation, we need a large enough doctrine of God – infinite and immeasurable transcendence, yet internally differentiated and interrelated trinity, and, above all, a personal God in a way that not only allows for incarnation but is in fact defined for us by incarnation.

Having followed Farrer's thought on the incarnate *deity*, and remembering his insistence in 'Very God and Very Man' that 'God, infinite God, no more ceases to be God by . . . being Jesus than he ceases to be God by making Jesus',[27] we now turn to the other pole of the doctrine of the Incarnation and consider the *humanity* of Christ.

Farrer's use of the abstract terms 'manhood' and 'humanity' may have made us suspicious on this score. But it would be quite wrong to suppose that Farrer really thought in terms of God taking abstract manhood into himself as opposed to coming amongst us as a particular individual man. On the contrary, we find him in *Saving Belief* saying 'This world is a world of accident, of sheer brute fact. If God was to put on a coat of flesh, the coat was sure to be made of casual stuff. He could not be a man-in-general. In fact he was a Galilean carpenter, turned freelance rabbi.'[28] Farrer obviously exulted in this paradox. The same words recur in a sermon to be found in *A Celebration of Faith*. Arguing that Jesus is not to be thought of as a god in masquerade, Farrer says, 'This was how God's love was shown as utterly divine – in accepting every circumstance of our manhood. He spared himself nothing. He was not a copybook man-in-general, he was a Galilean carpenter, a freelance rabbi; and he wove up his life, as each of us must, out of the materials that were to hand.'[29]

I should like to draw particular attention to two aspects of Farrer's understanding of the Incarnation which follow from the utter seriousness with which he takes the humanity of Christ. The first concerns human relatedness. Farrer is quite aware that to be a human person is to exist in personal relation to others. Jesus, he observes in a sermon (in *A Celebration of Faith*), was the Jesus he was because of his particular relations to others, to Mary and Joseph and the village rabbi – a man, Farrer notes, to us unknown.[30] The principle holds not only for Jesus' earthly life. 'Christ's incarnation', so we read in *Saving Belief*, 'would have been nothing, but for his relation to his family, his disciples and his nation; his continued incarnation, after he rose, would have been nothing, but for his continuing relation with those he left on earth. Presently they joined him, one by one, in glory; and so that mystical body was built up.'[31] The point is most fully expounded in *Love Almighty and Ills Unlimited*:

We speak of the incarnation of the Godhead, his taking of human flesh. Such a fashion of speech emphasises the height of the miracle, and the depth of the condescension. God brings an animal nature into personal identity with himself. But the flesh is not the point of union; the divine action does not fuse with the throbbing of Jesus' pulses; it fuses with the movement of his mind. And mind in man is a cultural or social fact. It cannot arise in isolation, and it has its natural being in mutual discourse. God could not become incarnate in a human vacuum, and neither can he remain incarnate so . . . Since he has been pleased to become incarnate, he needs the stuff and the embodiment which are involved in a true incarnation; that is, he needs the mystical Church.[32]

I suppose, incidentally, that that is as far as Farrer would go with the otherwise highly dubious notion of the Church as an extension of the Incarnation.

The second aspect I want to stress concerning the humanity of Christ is the limited nature of Jesus' knowledge. In the sermon on 'Incarnation' already quoted, Farrer asks 'What did Jesus know?' and replies 'He knew, initially, what a village boy learnt, who listened to the Rabbis and made the best of his opportunities.'[33] In *Faith and Speculation*, Farrer has much to say on the way in which the divine providence uses fallible human instruments. 'The paradigm', he says, 'is Christ's ability to play his part with a mental furniture acquired from his village rabbi.'[34] In *Saving Belief*, Farrer brings out the importance of a proper historical sense in viewing the humanity of Christ.

If God wished to make no more than any single one of us, he would need to make half a universe . . . He steered many sequences of cause, many lines of influence to their meeting place in you or in me. And so with the human being of Jesus . . . The Old Testament contains the story of God's secret providence in making the humanity of Christ.[35]

Farrer goes on to insist that we should see Jesus as

a Galilean villager of the first century. The tools of his thinking came from local stock; only he made a divinely perfect use of them. The Jewish ideas he inherited, broken and reshaped in the course of his life, served him for mental coinage, in the traffic of his unique sonship to his Father and his assertion of God's kingdom over mankind. He had what he needed to be the Son of God; as for defining the divine sonship, that was a task for other hands, using other tools.

This distinction was brought out most clearly in 'Very God and Very Man' with the help of Gilbert Ryle's distinction between knowing how and knowing that. Jesus did not know that he was God the Son. An omniscient being cannot be very man. But he knows how to be the Son of God in the several situations of his gradually unfolding destiny. 'God the Son on earth is a fullness of holy life within the limit of mortality.'[36]

I hope I have given sufficient evidence to show that a 'high' Christology such as Farrer's need have no 'docetic' tendencies. It represents a poverty of both imagination and theological grasp to suppose that the doctrine of the Incarnation is inevitably docetic.

Having said something about both deity and humanity in Farrer's understanding of the Incarnation, I should like to add a note about the difference between grace on the one hand and incarnation on the other. Farrer was quite clear about the difference. In a neat phrase from *Saving Belief* he says 'a good man helped by Grace may do human things divinely; Christ did divine things humanly.'[37] Generalising, Farrer goes on:

Wherever the eye of faith looks in the created world it perceives two levels of action. There is the creature making itself, and there is God making it make itself. Jesus is not unique in the mere fact that the personal life or act of God underlies his action; for nothing would either be or act, if God did not thus underlie it. But the underlying is not everywhere the same or (let us rather say) the relation between the underlying act of God, and the created energy overlaid upon it, is not everywhere the same relation. In the case of mere physical forces, there is the highest degree of mutual externality between the two; it is natural enough to speak of God's action here as the action of a cause. In the case of rational creatures, there is more mutual penetration; the entry of the divine into the human may be called inspiration on the one side, and co-operation on the other. In the person of Christ the mutual interpenetration is complete; it is necessary to talk of personal identity.

There is a very interesting passage in the chapter on 'Law and Spirit', where Farrer notes that 'it is the testimony of Scripture that Jesus himself was full of the Holy Ghost'.[38] But this does not mean 'two incompatible pictures of Christ: the Son of God by inspiration, the Son of God in nature and in person'. On the contrary, both are present in writers such as St John, who operate with the 'highest' Christologies in the New Testament. The reason for this, Farrer thinks, is their implicit recognition that the manner in which the incarnate Son is fulfilled with the Spirit reflects the Father's eternal indwelling of the Son by his Spirit. In other words, it is a mistake to contrast a 'spirit' Christology with an incarnational Christology, since the Spirit is active both in grace and incarnation. He is active in one way in us without making us personally identical with God; he is supremely active in the man Jesus, just because there a unique personal identity is brought about between the living centre of God and the human instrument of revelation and redemption.

This distinction is certainly asserted by Farrer, but one may well find oneself asking again why he thinks it must be pressed. It is not, he admits, a conclusion based simply on historical study. Athanasian dogma is not read off history alone, as Farrer says in 'Very God and Very Man'.[39] In addition to historical testimony, we have to reckon with a special kind of living testimony – the encounter by the disciples with the risen Christ, and Christian experience ever since. 'The evidence', says Farrer in a sermon in *Said or Sung*, 'that Jesus was God-from-God and God-with-God was that a life had come into the world which gave back to God the picture of his own face, and the love of his own heart. And the second evidence was the power of it.'[40] But we recall from our very first quotation from Farrer that in fact he found the justification in the exposition of the doctrine, the sense it makes of God and man and man's destiny. Thus the doctrine is most likely to be maintained when its scope and power are both seen and felt in a living Christian faith. As Farrer says in a sermon in *A Celebration of Faith*: 'God's love for us is that he comes to us. So the divine incarnation is our all-or-nothing. It is a pity, no doubt, that faith in Christ divides us from Jews and Turks; but the acknowledgement of vital truth is always divisive until it becomes universal.'[41]

I should like to conclude this survey of the doctrine of the Incarnation in the thought of Austin Farrer with two foot-notes, one on the Virgin Birth and the other on 'myth'.

In the sermon on 'Incarnation' Farrer states:

The virginal birth is not the substance of the Incarnation; it is the peculiar way in which (we have been told) it pleased God to bring it about. Jesus is not the Son of God *because* he had no human father. It would have been conceivable though it did not happen that the Son of God might have become incarnate as the offspring of an ordinary union.[42]

I do not know whether in 1961, when that sermon was preached in Keble College Chapel, Farrer might have had his tongue in his cheek with that 'we have been told'. Certainly he was disposed to accept the orthodox credal position, but, as we have seen, he wanted to understand it and expound it in a rational intelligible way, and it is significant that he recognises quite explicitly that the rationality of incarnational

123

belief does not necessarily commit one to the Virgin Birth. Moreover I find it interesting that the main thrust of Farrer's thought on the Incarnation is in the direction of seeing the Incarnation as the climax of and key to the operation of divine providence in the world, rather than a miraculous intervention out of the blue. Indeed it seems to me to be important to realise that the natural structures of the created world are not so alien to the Creator that they have to be broken or forced for him to enter into them and make himself present and knowable within them.

Finally a word on 'myth'. Farrer is a particularly important writer to consult on this topic, since he was a man of great poetic sensitivity and imagination. Like C. S. Lewis, he knew what myths are, and how they function in religion and literature. He was quite aware that the doctrine of the Incarnation looks mythical; nevertheless he held that actually it expresses supernatural fact. In an intriguing early essay, entitled 'Can Myth be Fact?' (to be found in *Interpretation and Belief*), he says: 'Men may construct a myth expressive of divine truths as they conceive them, and the stuff of that myth will be words. God has constructed a myth expressive of the living truths he intends to convey, and the stuff of the myth is facts.'[43] In other words God's story, God's parable, is a real human life and death. The language of Incarnation, then, is not just a human construct expressive of some general truth. It refers rather to God himself and his particular presence and act in our midst. The point is developed by Farrer in the 'Revelation' essay in *Faith and Logic*: 'We may call the Incarnation the self-enacted parable of Godhead, to express the belief that the existence and action of Christ are the divine translation, almost the symbolisation of the transcendent Life in human terms . . . The self-enacted parable of Godhead is parable relatively to the divine Being, but it is the very stuff of ours.'[44]

This seems to be a suitable place at which to close; for it

brings out very vividly the central insight, which we have seen expounded by Farrer in many different ways, that in the Incarnation we are confronted by 'infinite God, living the existence of one of his creatures, through self-limitation to a particular created destiny'. There can be little doubt that what Farrer is expounding here is the central tenet of historic Christianity, or that Farrer's lucid and profound exposition helps us to see the religious significance and force of incarnational belief. I have quoted so much Farrer verbatim in the hope that his words will also help us to see that the doctrine of the Incarnation really is a matter of insight rather than illusion.

10

Contemporary unitarianism

The most striking feature of recent British trinitarian theology – at least where England is concerned – is the frankness with which orthodox trinitarianism is being questioned or even rejected. This sceptical note in doctrinal criticism has also been sounded over the doctrine of the Incarnation – not surprisingly, for the two doctrines are, both historically and rationally, linked. Indeed the collapse of trinitarian theology is an inevitable consequence of the abandonment of incarnational Christology. Thus we find, in the writings of two Regius Professors of Divinity, at the Universities of Oxford and Cambridge, Maurice Wiles and Geoffrey Lampe, along with Christological reductionism, a marked tendency towards unitarianism. Neither Wiles nor Lampe can see much future for the doctrine of the Trinity.[1]

It is perfectly true that both scholars are prepared to go on using trinitarian language, and they would certainly unite in rejecting deistic versions of unitarianism whereby God is thought of as remote and isolated from the world. Both would stress the immanence of God in his creation. But neither is prepared to grant much meaning, let alone an essential place in Christian theism, to such classical formulations as that God is to be known and worshipped as three persons in one substance, or even to the looser affirmation that there exist relations of love within God.

Both Wiles and Lampe are liberal theologians. They have

126

affinities with turn-of-the-century German 'liberal Protestantism', as exemplified in the writings of Harnack and
Troeltsch; but they are more characteristically English
scholars and have more in common with the 'Modern
Churchmen', whose Girton Conference of 1921 caused such
a stir in British religious circles more than a generation ago.
They share the clarity, the common sense and the rationalism
of Bethune-Baker and Hastings Rashdall.

It is notable that Wiles and Lampe are both primarily
patristic scholars. They are at home in the arguments of the
early Christian Fathers, and yet have come to reject them on
matters which they, the Fathers, thought to be central to, and
of the essence of, the Christian faith. It is also true to say that
both scholars sit pretty lightly to the traditions of dogma,
whether Catholic, Lutheran or Reformed, that come between
the patristic age and our own.

There are differences between the two theologians. For one
thing, Wiles' doctrinal criticism has been developed and
sustained over a longer period of time and, one senses, in
reaction against a once-held conservative theology of the
Word. He restricts himself to hard-headed theological argument, relentlessly pressing the questions of meaning and
truth. Lampe has moved more rapidly in recent years to an
affirmation of minimal dogma, but from a long-held liberal
Catholic position that is still sustained by sacramental piety.
There is, in the Bampton Lectures, for all their critical stance
towards the doctrines of the Incarnation and the Trinity, a
wealth of mature spiritual insight.

Clarity is a great virtue, and the writings of Professors
Wiles and Lampe are a pleasure to read. It is easy to understand what they are saying. There is no resort to rhetoric or
bluster. The contrast between this calm reflective English
theology and the dense and convoluted prose of many continental writers is very great. Yet the German theologians,
with the major exception of the Bultmann school, and not-

withstanding their awareness of the need to take the measure of Bultmann, remain obstinately, even excitingly, trinitarian. This is true of both Protestant and Catholic theology in Germany today. It is one of the ironies of the present theological scene that Liberal Protestantism has found a new lease of life in England at a time when it seems to have run its course in Germany.

This contrast between the clear and reasonable unitarianism of recent English theology and the dense and opaque trinitarianism of German theology has not always obtained. An earlier Oxford professor, Leonard Hodgson, writing with just such clarity, common sense and rationalism as are displayed by Wiles and Lampe, found himself driven to accept and to commend an orthodox trinitarian theology. 'The doctrine of the Trinity', he wrote,

is the product of rational reflection on those particular manifestations of the divine activity which centre in the birth, ministry, crucifixion, resurrection and ascension of Jesus Christ, and the gift of the Holy Spirit to the Church . . . it could not have been discovered without the occurrence of those events, which drove human reason to see that they required a trinitarian God for their cause.[2]

In discussing the work of Wiles and Lampe, we need to ask two main questions: in the first place, what are the reasons for their rejection of the trinitarian tradition? Secondly, how adequate are their non-trinitarian concepts of God? Or, put the other way round, what is lost from Christian theism when we cease to think in trinitarian terms?

The fact that these are the questions I wish to put to Wiles and Lampe shows that, to some extent, at least, I share their approach to theological problems. The doctrine of the Trinity cannot be established simply by citing authoritative texts, whether of scripture or tradition. Its primary source is certainly divine revelation, but, as Leonard Hodgson saw, revelation is a matter of events, of divine actions in human history and in human lives. Revelation is not opposed to reason. Part of our response to God's self-revealing acts is precisely our rational reflection on the sense they make.

Already we are concerned with theological method, and consideration of my first question – What are the reasons for Wiles' and Lampe's dissatisfaction with the doctrine of the Trinity? – must begin with the problem of method. So far I have expressed agreement. We cannot take this doctrine simply on authority. But when we look more closely at the work of Wiles and Lampe, doubts on the score of method begin to arise. It is Wiles who addresses himself most explicitly to problems of theological method, but similar procedures can be detected as being implicit in the work of Lampe as well. In *The Remaking of Christian Doctrine*, Wiles tells us that the two words that best describe his objective are 'coherence' and 'economy'.[3] I have no quarrel with the criterion of coherence, though I shall argue shortly that Lampe, at least, too readily supposes trinitarian theology to be incoherent. My chief worry concerns 'economy'. The use of this criterion is pervasive in both Wiles and Lampe. We are not to postulate more doctrine than the evidence *demands*. It was not *necessary* for the Fathers to erect the doctrinal superstructure that they did in the way they did. Here are two examples from Lampe: 'In order to interpret God's saving work in Jesus we do not need the model of a descent of a pre-existent divine person into the world'; 'If . . . it is God's Spirit, his own real presence, which is active in and through the reciprocal love and trust of human beings, then there is no need to project human personality on to Trinitarian "persons".'[4] I shall discuss the substance of this last quotation later on. Here it simply illustrates the common use of the criterion of 'economy'. We are to cut out all unnecessary theological accretions. This is a very dangerous criterion, especially when used alone. It is not surprising that, on this ground, unitarianism is preferred.

My objection is not to the criterion of economy as such,

however. We should indeed consider what the evidence demands. Leonard Hodgson, in the passage quoted above, argued that the revelatory events *drove* human reason to see that they required a trinitarian God for their cause. My objection rather is to stress on economy to the neglect of comprehensiveness. Before we appeal to what the evidence demands, we must be sure that we are taking account of *all* the evidence, that all the data are being scrutinised in all their relevant aspects. It is an objection to Wiles' method that he tends to take a particular patristic argument in isolation, show that it was not *necessary* to think that way, and conclude that Christian theology would be better off without that particular doctrine. But by such a procedure one can easily miss much relevant evidence, and overlook the real reasons behind the Fathers' thinking. Considerations of economy and considerations of comprehensiveness must be weighed together. Nor is it just a question of historical evidence. It is a further objection to Wiles' use of his criterion of economy – though this does not apply to Lampe – that Wiles tends to think historically rather than theologically about the development of doctrine. We are to accept only what seems necessary to account for the historical evidence. But this is to neglect theological considerations – theological judgement on what the Fathers were doing, and theological reflection on the implications of the religious tradition in which one is oneself participating.

What are the reasons, other than those of method, why dissatisfaction with trinitarian theology is being expressed today? A word should be said about Wiles' other criterion, 'coherence'. Here it is Lampe who confesses most explicitly doubts about the coherence of the doctrine of the Trinity, especially where, with Leonard Hodgson, the 'social analogy' is pressed, and real relations are postulated within the deity. Lampe cannot see how this can be anything other than tritheism. But that betrays a strange insensitivity to the Christian tradition. There is no question of Christian trinitarian belief involving belief in three gods. As I have argued eleswhere,[5] in trinitarian theology we are speaking of the internal self-differentiation of the one infinite source of all created being. Relations within the Blessed Trinity are not external relations. I shall insist below that we have to postulate relation *in* God if we are to make sense of the relation of God incarnate to God the Father, and also if we are to make sense of the central Christian affirmation that God is love. This means that we cannot possibly model our understanding of a personal God on an isolated individual. But neither can we model it, equally anthropomorphically, on two or three such individuals externally related. The accusation of tritheism betrays such an anthropomorphic conception of one's opponents' views. It does not begin to do justice to the careful trinitarian theology characteristic of the mainstream Christian tradition. St Thomas Aquinas, for example, combines in a most creative way the insights of the 'psychological analogy', suggestive of internal self-projection, and the 'social analogy', suggestive of real subsistent relations in God.[6] If we find such theology incoherent, we must ask ourselves, before we reject it, whether we are not ourselves in bondage to an over-literal, anthropomorphic, picture of what the other is trying to say.

I am not suggesting that it is easy to articulate an understanding of God in Trinity. It is, of course, even more difficult for us today to do this than it was for our predecessors in the faith. Aquinas could simply assume the doctrine as authoritatively given, and then spell out its rationality and force. He performed the latter task with unparalleled acuteness. But *we* must at the same time make the case for thinking in trinitarian terms at all. We cannot just assume it as something given. Leonard Hodgson grasped this problem with admirable forthrightness, but no one should underestimate its difficulty. We should remember that we are letting Christian experience of Christ and the Spirit drive us on to postulate something strictly inaccessible to finite human minds, something about the infinite transcendent life of God in its fullness and richness of love given and love received, a mystery which we cannot and ought not to presume to be able to articulate precisely. Yet the fact that we, unlike our predecessors, have to argue the case for trinitarian belief, as well as spell out its rationality, has at least this advantage: it enables us to see more clearly the crucial features of Christian experience that led to trinitarian belief in the first place, and still sustains it today. To my mind there are three such crucial features, which require us to resist the slide towards unitarianism. They are (1) recognition of the divinity of Christ, of Christ as alive with the life of God, and as manifesting through his relation to the Father the inner relation of love given and love received in God; (2) recognition that the Spirit of God in our hearts is not a matter of undifferentiated divine immanence, but rather of one who gathers us up into God's own inner life and inner dialogue; and (3) recognition that God *is* love, not just that he loves us, but that love – and that means love given and love received – is of the essence of his inner being.

I note this threefold recognition, as well as admission of the difficulty of articulating it much further, in Professor C. F. D. Moule's recent study, *The Holy Spirit*.[7] Moule somewhat ruefully quotes Lampe's disparaging remarks about the traditional technical terminology of 'generation' and 'procession' in the Trinity. (Aquinas, incidentally, speaks of two 'processions', differentiating the 'generation' of the Son from the 'spiration' of the Spirit.) Well, maybe we can sit fairly lightly to this terminology. But there was no harm in the early Fathers and their successors having invented labels for the twofold self-projection of God, which Christians have discerned as lying behind their twofold experience of Christ and the Spirit.

Let us now turn to the second of my questions to Professors

Wiles and Lampe. How adequate are their non-trinitarian concepts of God? What is lost when we cease to think in trinitarian terms? In the article referred to in note 5, I suggested that Wiles' concept of God is that much vaguer, the more he retreats from the differentiations of traditional trinitarian and incarnational theology. He is reduced to affirming the 'richness and complexity' of God's being, without being able to justify this assertion, let alone say anything about it. This accusation may appear to rebound upon my own head; for have I not myself just been saying that precision is impossible where talk of the ultimate mystery of God is concerned? But Christian talk of God as the Blessed Trinity is given its measure of precision, in contrast with other talk of God, precisely through the self-revealing acts which drive us to postulate a trinitarian God in the first place. We think precisely of God when we think of the love of Jesus for the Father and the Father's love for his only-begotten Son, when we think of the way God takes human life and suffering and death into himself in the passion and Cross of Christ, when we think of the way in which, as Paul puts it in Romans 8, 'the Spirit of God searches our inmost being . . . pleading for God's people in God's own way', and when we think of our Christian life and worship as being caught up into the trinitarian life of God.

Wiles has also, somewhat unjustly, been accused of deism; for his conception of divine action in the world seems pale and insubstantial compared with the biblical picture of the acts of God. Wiles prefers the language of 'immanence', 'purpose' and 'presence'. Certainly, in philosophical theology, we must be careful not to reduce divine activity to the operation of one cause among others at the same level (except where God himself makes that reduction in incarnation). We have to think of the divine activity as an utterly different dimension of activity, working in and through creatures. On this score, Lampe's conception of God as Spirit has much to recommend it. Lampe is

133

extremely sensitive to the mediated activity of God as Spirit in human lives. Yet one has to say that this conception of Spirit remains rather vague, and is certainly unanalysed. Deprived of its anchorage in incarnational Christology and in the differentiated experience of the Spirit described by Paul, it fails to provide much real content for our knowledge of God. Its whole meaning seems to be exhausted when spelt out in terms of some sense of being inspired. This sense of God is common among many religions and should not be undervalued. But it is hard to see how such a transcendent/immanent Spirit can really be thought of in personal terms, especially when this God is no longer thought of relationally.

This brings me to the chief objection which I want to make against Lampe's theology. Lampe argues, in a passage from which I have already quoted, that there is no need to posit relation in God, since a God who is immanent in all creation enjoys all the reciprocities of personal relation in and through his creatures as he creates them from within. I am afraid that this to me sounds very much like whistling in the dark. If God depends on his creation for the enjoyment of the perfection of personal relation, then it seems that God is being thought of as dependent on his creation for being personal at all. And if the personality of God depends on creatures, what sort of God is it that we are really thinking of? This is the impasse into which all forms of unitarianism are led, and it stands out here in Lampe's book all the more blatantly for the clarity of its unashamed admission. The great tradition of Christian trinitarian theology stood under no such illusion. St Thomas Aquinas, writing in the thirteenth century, answers Lampe's argument precisely with a homely parable. Considering the objection that God is not alone because he is with angels and the souls of the blessed, he replies:

Although angels and the souls of the blessed are always with God, nevertheless it would follow that God was alone or solitary if there were not several divine persons. For the company of something of a quite different nature does not end solitude, and so we say that a man is alone in the garden although there are in it many plants and animals.[8]

The point is the converse of Genesis 2.18, where God, having created Adam, and despite his own discourse with Adam, says 'it is not good that man should be alone', and creates Eve to be a helper fit for him. Perhaps this is the place at which we might recall another point, expressed in Karl Barth's creative exegesis of the Genesis 1 creation narrative. There God says, 'Let us make man in our image, after our likeness.' 'So God created man in his own image, in the image of God he created him; male and female he created them.' Barth saw this recognition of man's essentially relational nature as pointing to the essentially relational nature of the one in whose image man and woman were made.[9]

As I write these things I am conscious yet again of Lampe's fears of tritheism and of the dangers of the 'social analogy'. In recalling my earlier repudiation of this fear, I should add that we must not allow the human side of the analogy to dominate our grasp of the divine side. If human persons exist in relation only externally, over against other individuals, this is precisely *not* the feature to be extrapolated into God. The argument should proceed the other way round. It is because Christians believe that God exists in the fullness of relation – love given and love received – within the oneness of his own infinite being that they also believe that man's individuality and externality will one day be overcome.

What then is lost from Christian theism when we cease to think in trinitarian terms? I can only sum up by expanding on the points already made. The conviction that God is love is the major casualty of unitarian theism. Of course it cuts corners to say, with Hans Urs von Balthasar, 'God *is* Love and therefore Trinity.'[10] The argument should run: God *is* Love and therefore in himself relational, the perfection of love given and love received. The threefoldness of God cannot be inferred apart from the gifts of Christ and the Spirit. But might the relatedness of God have been inferred apart from the gifts of Christ and the Spirit, simply through reflection on the love of God? Well, I think it might, given the premise that God is love. Yet it is not an obvious datum that God is love. That premise of relational thinking about God is itself a hard-won insight. It appears in other faiths, admittedly – in devotional Hinduism, for instance; indeed one often finds the Hindu god provided with a consort. (That really is anthropomorphic theology.) But the kind of basic common factor which writers on religion such as Rudolf Otto have found in the theistic faiths – the numinous, the holy – is not easily identified as love. There is too much evil in the world and in human relationships to allow an easy reading of the source of all things in terms of love. The Johannine affirmation that God is love itself arose out of conviction that the nature of God had been revealed not only in the Passion and the Cross of the incarnate Word, but in the relation between the Father and the Son. So the full conviction that God is love, like conviction that God is three in one, arises after all from reflection on the self-revealing costly acts of God in Christ. Nor can we say that, in response to revelation, reason discerns the triunity while the heart discerns the love of God. For the *rationality* of talk of God as love is at stake. The burden of my argument against Wiles and Lampe has been that we can no longer rationally think of God as love when relational – in Christian terms, trinitarian – thinking goes by the board.

The other losses of non-trinitarian religion are of a piece with this major casualty. Christ becomes one inspired man among others; and the Spirit a universal divine immanence within creation. We no longer have a living Saviour, by incorporation into whose Body we too can say 'Abba, Father'; we no longer can think of our prayers and worship as taken up into the inner movement of God's life. I am inclined to think too that a residual conviction of personality in God lives off the capital of past trinitarian belief.

Discussion has been restricted in this essay to the work of two leading English scholars, whose virtual unitarianism undoubtedly marks one strand in recent British theology. There are other names that could be mentioned as exemplifying the same tendency. But the balance must be redressed a little at the end, if the impression is not to be given that British theology as a whole has moved in this direction. Quite the reverse is true of the leading figure in Scottish theology, Professor T. F. Torrance, winner of the 1978 Templeton Prize for Progress in Religion. Torrance has thrown a great deal of light, in his voluminous writings, on the doctrines of the Incarnation and of the Spirit, and thereby on the specifically Christian trinitarian form of belief in God.

In England, trinitarian theology has been ably expounded by David Jenkins, who shows how the vision and understanding of God which is symbolised by the Trinity sets us free to take love absolutely seriously. Three Cambridge professors may also be mentioned, whose sense of the importance and the rationality of Christian trinitarian theology constitutes a significant counterbalance to the work of Wiles and Lampe. I have already referred to C. F. D. Moule's study on *The Holy Spirit*. His earlier lectures on Christology demonstrated the grounding of a relational view of God already in New Testament times, and the continuity between the New Testament and the early Councils of the Church. Sympathy for the achievement of the Fathers in respect of the ontology of God is shown by G. C. Stead in his book, *Divine Substance*. Of particular interest is his refutation of certain philosophical criticisms of the use of the concept of 'substance' in theology and Christology. Finally, an essay by the Scottish philosopher of religion, D. M. MacKinnon, in the Festschrift for T. F. Torrance may be mentioned, and indeed quoted as a fitting conclusion to the argument of this essay. Citing Oliver Quick's remark that he regarded as the very touchstone of orthodoxy the frankly mythological clause in the creed – *descendit de coelis* ('he came down from heaven') – MacKinnon writes: 'What is the doctrine of the Trinity if not the effort so to reconstruct the doctrine of God that this "descent" may be seen as supremely, indeed, paradigmatically, declaratory of what He is in himself?'[11]

11
'True' and 'false' in Christology

It may seem a far cry from contemporary philosophical analysis of the meaning of the word 'true' to the solemn use of the concept of truth in the Fourth Gospel. There the writer places on the lips of Jesus words which express his own profound conviction that the ultimate truth of God and man is revealed, indeed embodied, in the figure of Jesus himself. Before Pilate, Jesus says, 'To this end was I born, and for this cause came I into the world, that I should bear witness unto the truth.' Earlier he had said to the disciples: 'If ye continue in my word, then are ye my disciples indeed; and ye shall know the truth, and the truth shall make you free.' Similarly in the farewell discourses, he says of the Comforter, 'When he, the Spirit of truth is come, he will guide you into all truth . . . He shall glorify me, for he shall receive of mine and shall shew it unto you.' And of course, most concretely of all: 'I am the way, the truth and the life'.[1] But in reflecting on these pronouncements, the philosophical theologian is bound to ask himself what is the relation between the ordinary uses of the word 'true' and these profound religious uses.

The conception of personal truth which we find in the Fourth Gospel is very different from the 'personal truth' advocated by Wilfred Cantwell Smith.[2] The Jesus of the Fourth Gospel is not just speaking of a quality of personal living, by comparison with which the truth of doctrines fades into insignificance. On the contrary, embedded in the religious pronouncements of the Fourth Gospel about truth lie deep convictions about how things ultimately are with God, man and the world and about how man and the world were meant to be. These convictions can and must be expressed in propositional form, as 'proposals for belief'.[3] Consequently, analysis of the meaning of the word 'true', as used in these far-reaching religious contexts, is a necessary task for philosophical theology.

It is most unlikely that the analysis of truth in religious contexts advocated by D. Z. Phillips will be found to do justice to the pronouncements of the Fourth Gospel.[4] For Phillips, 'truth' and 'reality' are not general terms whose meaning can be fixed, irrespective of context. The sense of 'truth' and 'reality' in religion can be determined only within the religious 'language-game'. There is no analogy between everyday truth or scientific truth and truth in religion. Internal criteria alone can show what it means to speak of religious truth. I do not think that this analysis does justice to what ordinary believers mean when they affirm the truth of their beliefs. As a number of philosophers have pointed out,[5] we have here a dispute that could in principle be settled by phenomenological or sociological research. Equally, a careful reading of the Fourth Gospel will support the view that, even in the solemn passages quoted above, the word 'true' is being used in its basic, common, sense of that which expresses or shows how things really are and were meant to be.

Before considering the specific question of 'true' and 'false' in Christology, I want to explore this more general question of the nature of truth. Theories of meaning and truth are much debated in contemporary secular philosophy, as indeed are the underlying metaphysical conceptions of reality that explicitly or implicitly accompany them. No doubt it is impolitic for theology too exclusively to endorse particular – and highly controversial – philosophical theories. But the case I wish to state and examine at this stage is the threefold thesis that meaning is to be understood in terms of a combination of truth-conditions and the intentions of rational minds, that truth is to be understood in terms of that which expresses or shows how things really are and were meant to be, and that reality is to be understood in terms first of the being and nature of God and then of a universe with a given nature and destiny which we discover rather than invent or construct.

The concepts of meaning, truth and reality are closely bound up together. We specify the meaning of an assertion or belief, at least in part, by indicating what it would be for that assertion or belief to be true. We specify, that is, its truth-conditions. But assertions and beliefs are states or acts of knowing minds, and neither meaning nor truth can be defined apart from reference to the mind. A statement, a gesture, an event only means something to someone. Equally, truth is the disclosure of reality to the mind and the expression of how things are by rational minds for rational minds.

This does not mean that how things are depends on *our* minds. For the theist, God is who he is and the world is what it is irrespective of our knowing minds. On the other hand, the world's reality does depend on the mind and will of God. In this sense, the world and man are mind-dependent. They depend on God for their being, their nature and their destiny. This is the element of truth in the metaphysical theory known as idealism. But of course philosophical idealism has tended rather to assert the dependence of the world on *our* minds. This is the dominant characteristic of those post-Kantian strands in western philosophy, which, losing confidence in the objectivity of God and his creation, have tended greatly to exaggerate the contribution of the human mind to the constitution of how things are. Phenomenalism and other forms of idealism are united in opposing the view that things are what they are independently of specifically human ways of knowing and of human powers of verification. This is equally true of the most popular form of anti-realism today, the philosophical position or cluster of positions known as constructivism, whereby the objects of our thought and discourse are held to be constituted by our socially constructed projections, categorical frameworks and webs of meaning.

Against these theories, metaphysical realism insists that the world is what it is irrespective of *our* knowing minds. We discover rather than constitute reality. Christian theism asserts the given nature of the realities which we come to apprehend. God gives himself to be known by us in revelation and he gives the world its nature and rational structure which we discover through interacting with it both in everyday life and in science. Further, just because the world is in process, we need to discern not only how things are but where they are going. Not only the present reality of the world, but also its future, according to Christian theism, is governed by the divine intention. We have also, therefore, to discover what it was meant to be.

One of the merits of theism is that it makes it possible to retain the connection between reality, truth and knowability without either according implausible powers to our human minds or collapsing into scepticism. Plato held categorically that ultimate reality was entirely knowable by us, and in his exaggerated confidence in the scope of philosophy, believed the supreme realities to be accessible to any properly trained mind.[6] Heidegger, more realistically for a non-theistic philosopher, held that the being of things was hidden and concealed, and only came to expression fitfully and enigmatically in poetry and in a philosophy that rejected most of its own past.[7] Karl Jaspers was even more pessimistic about our ability to know transcendent being. For him, metaphysics, religion and poetry all provide no more than 'ciphers' of an essentially unknowable and inexpressible transcendence.[8] By contrast with the excessive optimism of Plato and the excessive pessimism of Heidegger and Jaspers, Christian theism has retained the conviction of the inseparability of reality, truth and knowability, without supposing ourselves to be capable of knowing all there is to be known. It is enabled to do this by its postulation of God's knowledge as alone commensurate with how things really are. But God's knowledge of what he has made and God's creative power ensure the objectivity and stability of what there is for us, with our limited powers of cognition, to come at least partially to know.

Michael Dummett has pointed out the close connection between anti-realist metaphysics and verificationist theories of meaning and truth, whereby only what is in principle verifiable *by us* can have any claim to truth-content.[9] A theory which grounds objective truth and knowability in the mind and will of God frees the notions of meaning and truth from that anthropocentric verificationism which characterise those post-Kantian phenomenalist or constructivist philosophies mentioned above.

There are interesting possibilities of *argument* for theism here. For if we can defend the notion of objective reality being what it is independently of human minds, and there for us to discover as we aim at truth, only on the supposition of its knowability by transcendent mind, then perhaps there is a rational argument from truth to God. At first sight this looks a viciously circular argument. Are we not appealing to objective truth as a ground for belief in God and at the same time to God as a guarantor of objective truth? But I do not think that the argument is circular. For I notice that in everyday life and in science alike, we find an enormous resistance to idealist, phenomenalist and constructivist ways of thinking. Working scientists, for the most part, think of themselves as probing the secrets of a universe that exists over against them, with a structure and a rationality which are not imposed by the human mind, but rather discovered through interaction by trial and error, between the scientist and his subject matter, a structure and a rationality that may well exceed our human powers of comprehension. If it is the case that our experience of the world prompts this realist view of objective

143

truth, then, perhaps, a springboard for theistic argument is achieved.

As in other spheres, Nietzsche was more perceptive about what is at issue here than many modern philosophers, and indeed some modern theologians. His rejection of the notions of absolute and objective truth was part and parcel of his rejection of Christian theism. As in the ethical sphere, Nietzsche's explicit avowal of the consequences of atheism – in this case, complete relativism and the theory of truth as fiction – is perhaps an indication of the fact that objective truth and theism belong together.[10]

Turning to the theory of truth that most readily reflects the metaphysical and theological realism which I have been defending, I want now to consider the merits and demerits of the correspondence theory of truth, as a general theory capable of covering all the diverse uses of 'true' in everyday talk, in interpersonal discourse, in historical research, in science and in religion. In its most general form, the correspondence theory of truth is surely unassailable and indispensable. It affirms that a statement, belief or theory is true just when it expresses or shows how things are in reality. It does not necessarily involve the view, which the early Wittgenstein held, that statements somehow picture states of affairs, still less the view that there is a one-to-one correlation between words and things or between sentences and states of affairs. All that is needed is Aristotle's basic definition: 'To say of what is that it is not, or of what is not that it is, is false, while to say of what is that it is, and of what is not that it is not, is true.'[11] In other words, truth is correctly predicated of statements, opinions, beliefs, claims, theories, etc., when reality is in fact as they hold it to be. The basic claim of the correspondence theory, then, is that truth is a relation between the knowing mind and how things really are.

The problem with the correspondence theory lies in the difficulty and complexity – at least for creatures such as ourselves – of articulating and expressing in our own human thought and language how things are. This difficulty can be brought out if we begin with simple everyday cases such as saying truly of my hat that it is on the peg and moving rapidly on to more complex subjects such as interpersonal relations, historical judgements, scientific knowledge and religious awareness. In the simple everyday cases it is clear that all we need are conventions of reference, so that we succeed in picking out my hat as the object of discourse, and conventions of description or predication, so that we succeed in saying that it is on the peg. It seems *prima facie* reasonable to presume that we shall continue to need conventions of successful reference and appropriate predication when we move on to the more complex areas of discourse. The trouble is that that they are much more difficult to achieve. It has become increasingly apparent to philosophers and sociologists of knowledge that many of the things we say about the world are only partly or roughly true, and, moreover, are bound up with whole conceptual frameworks and ways of looking at the world which are highly conditioned historically, culturally and socially. This has led to widespread scepticism about our ability to say how things are in themselves, irrespective of our human modes of apprehension. These difficulties, however, need not deflect us from a correspondence theory of truth as broadly defined in its most general form above. For we can still suppose that humanly conditioned theories aim at truth in the fully objective sense of correspondence with reality. Awareness of the partial, approximate, theory-laden and often distorted nature of our affirmations need not deter us from the aim of discovering and bringing to expression how things are.

This analysis applies no less in the sphere of religion than it does in other spheres of human interest. Our aim, in religious discourse, is to bring to expression how things ultimately are with man, the universe and God. Of course the subject-matter of religion is such that we shall not be able to

145

rest content even with the partial articulation of how things ultimately *are*. Since we are now talking about, among other things, the will of God for man and the world, we shall no doubt find ourselves endeavouring to express how things were meant to be as well. We have already had occasion to turn to this extension of the theory of truth at earlier stages in this essay and we shall naturally be developing it when we return to the question of 'true' and 'false' in Christology. Suffice it to say here that the correspondence theory of truth is not over-thrown when we extend its scope from characterising the relation between the knowing mind and things as they are to characterising the relation between the knowing mind and things as they were meant to be. Objectivity is secured both for actual and intended truth by reference to the creative will of God.

It will be apparent that, for all spheres of discourse, the broad correspondence theory of truth defended here is quite capable of embracing recent philosophical theories of mean-ing and truth which stress the 'holistic' or 'network' character of human modes of representing how things are. Only when allied to constructivist, non-realist, *metaphysical* theories of the kind referred to above are these theories inimical to the con-ception of truth sketched here.

In summary, we may suggest that in all spheres of thought and discourse, human minds inherit and refine ways of representing to themselves and to each other, however par-tially and approximately, how things are. In discovering how things are, they become aware of a world in process, with a given structure, about which they learn more and more, always aiming at truth in the sense of that which expresses or shows how things are. Led beyond this objective truth to its source in the mind and will of God, they may hope to learn something of the divine intention for the world and man, and so progress to the question of how things were meant to be. The concept of truth is then deployed within a larger horizon, as we endeavour to articulate not only present truth, but future truth and ideal truth too, in the light of God's intention.

This larger horizon will naturally come into focus as we turn now to the question of 'true' and 'false' in Christology, and especially when we come back to the pronouncements of the Fourth Gospel with which this essay began. But Christology, as a branch of Christian theology – that is, as a reflective, second-order discipline – is not itself a matter of religious pronouncements. It is rather the attempt to analyse and articulate the doctrine implicit in the Church's witness to Jesus Christ, including the pronouncements of the Fourth Gospel. It is therefore just as much concerned with present truth as it is with future or ideal truth. It is concerned both to state, as carefully and fully as human language permits, who Christ is and what he reveals about the being and nature of God, and also to state, as carefully and fully as human language permits, what he reveals and embodies of God's intention for man and for the world. The remainder of this chapter is devoted to these two aspects of Christology and their claim to truth.

It is an implication of the main theme of this chapter that, when the Christian theologian claims that the doctrines of the Trinity and the Incarnation are true – that they state truly how things are with God and Jesus Christ – he is using the word 'true' in the same basic, common, sense as that in which it is used in any other sphere of discourse. These doctrines, he holds, correspond with reality. What is special about these doctrines is not the sense in which they are held to be true, but rather their peculiar subject-matter and the difficulty, for human beings, of cognitive access to it. Of course, the theologian does not hold that these doctrines tell us the whole truth about God and Jesus Christ. He is perfectly well aware that the realities into cognitive relation with which they put us are much greater and more mysterious than we can comprehend.

147

But this transcendence of the reality of God over all our modes of apprehension, including the doctrines of the Church, does not mean that the doctrines in question are false. We do not have to have complete comprehension of every aspect of the being and nature of God in order to make *some* true affirmations about him. In fact, human beings do not have complete comprehension of every aspect of any reality with which they have to do, but this does not prevent them from making some true statements about many things. Each reality, even a stone, transcends our ways of apprehending it, as both scientists and mystics have observed. But that does not prevent many true remarks being made about the stone.

Nor does the partial and approximate nature of our grasp of truth mean that the distinction between true and false statements is eroded, either in simple cases such as talk of stones or in complex cases such as talk of God. An intermediate example, talk of other people, may be used to illustrate this point. When I say that X is an honourable man, the complexity of my subject-matter, a human being and his character, no doubt transcends my relatively simple remark. (I deliberately choose an example of evaluation. Such remarks are clearly true or false. There are recognised criteria of what is to count as consistent honourable conduct.) But my remark may very well be true and be known to be true, none the less. A malicious rumour to the effect that X is a dishonourable man would, in that case, be false. The conventions of successful reference (I am talking about X, not Y) and of appropriate predication ('honourable' is rightly predicated of X, not 'dishonourable') are not rendered impotent by the difficulty of knowing the full truth about a man. Similarly, in the much more complex case of talk of God, if I say that, in one of the modes of his triune being, God became man in Jesus of Nazareth, I may be speaking truly, notwithstanding the much greater difficulty of making successful reference to

148

the subject of my affirmation (the triune God, not Wotan) and of appropriately predicating something of him (that, in one of the modes of his being, he became man, not that he was busy completing Valhalla).

In this difficult and complex sphere, it may not always be so easy to identify incompatible claims as it is in the examples I have given, let alone to say which has the greater claim to truth. This is true both of disputes within a particular religious tradition, and still more of disputes between religions as they come to expression through comparative study or through inter-faith dialogue. In neither case should we assume that *prima facie* differences represent irreconcilably conflicting truth-claims. It is a prime task in comparative theology to search out what common ground there may be behind the apparently different religions. Consideration of the many-sided nature of divine reality and of the different cultural and historical backgrounds to the conceptual frameworks in terms of which different traditions endeavour to articulate their experience of God may well enable us to resolve some *prima facie* incompatibilities and recognise a single reality lying behind the different modes of apprehension. P. T. Geach, in a well-known article,[12] has argued forcefully against any easy assimilations here, but he shows insufficient sensitivity to the possibility that, beneath the differences, there remains some more or less vague apprehension of the same reality. It may well be admitted that the price of agreement in these matters is often greater vagueness. Moreover some incompatibilities may well remain. Participants in inter-faith dialogue may reluctantly be driven to insist that some at least of the proposals put forward for acceptance by their partners in dialogue actually contradict their own beliefs. Here questions of truth and falsehood cannot be avoided.[13]

Much the same situation obtains within a single tradition. Recent christological controversy within Christian theology illustrates this. Admittedly there is less disagreement here about the referents of Christian discourse. We are all talking about the God of the Christians and about Jesus of Nazareth. What is in dispute is what is said of these subjects. The controversial area is that of appropriate predication. But, as in the case of the dialogue between religions, it is important to search out what common ground there may be behind the christological disputes. Apparently different proposals for belief in this area too may turn out, on closer inspection, to be conveying in different ways the same underlying doctrine. For example, proponents of incarnational and non-incarnational Christology respectively may be brought to agree on the central significance for Christianity of Paul's affirmation that 'God was in Christ, reconciling the world to Himself'.[14] But the price of such agreement is likely, once again, to be a greater measure of vagueness. By contrast, when pressed on what he understands this Pauline affirmation to mean, the incarnational christologian will insist that Christ must be thought of as coming to us from the side of God, the ultimate subject of his words and deeds being God himself in one of the modes of his triune being, while the non-incarnational christologian will suggest it is enough to speak of God's unique acts by his Spirit in and through the man, Jesus of Nazareth. So it may well turn out that the disagreements are deep ones after all. The rival Christologies cannot both be true, even though both parties have *some* awareness of the religious realities whose more specific interpretation is in dispute.

I detect in the arguments of recent proponents of non-incarnational Christology both an implicit trading on the greater vagueness of the agreed statements held in common, such as the Pauline affirmation quoted above, and at the same time an explicit defence of a less vague but definitely non-incarnational interpretation of such statements. These disputes raise interesting questions about the use of 'true' and 'false' in Christology. Vague statements can certainly be true or false, in any sphere of discourse ('There's something in the cupboard'). And if we were right to emphasise the partial and approximate nature of all human awareness, we shall expect relative degrees of vagueness in all statements about any subject-matter. No doubt religious statements are more prone to vagueness than many others. They employ many extended and figurative modes of expression – analogy, metaphor, symbol, parable, myth – modes of expression which are certainly not equivalent, and all of which are open to scrutiny and analysis. The distinction between 'true' and 'false' is perfectly applicable to all these modes of discourse as well as to the attempts at more specific doctrinal interpretation of what they convey. But a vaguely grasped truth may, when explored more precisely, come to be falsely interpreted. As in all spheres, in religion too, the scope for error becomes greater the more specific the articulation. This is not a reason for resting content with vague generalities about which we can all agree. For it may be the case that the religious power of Christianity depends on relatively precise beliefs about Jesus Christ being true.

So far I have only referred to certain basic doctrines about the person of Christ. No doubt it is much more important for Christian theology to articulate the moral truths about God's nature and providence, embodied and enacted in Christ and his Cross. But my point is that to see the Cross of Christ as God's Cross in our world implies the incarnational Christology. The moral truths and the doctrinal truths are inseparable. This means that the question of future truth and ideal truth – the question, that is, of what the world and man were meant to be – are also questions of christological doctrine. Christology is not only concerned with Christ as the human face of God, but also with Christ as the pattern of what man was meant to be. The will of God for the world and for man comes to expression in the incarnate one.

These reflections lead us to recognise the all-important fact

151

for a proper analysis of the use of the term 'true' in Christology that truth is not only expressed and shown in statements and beliefs, but is also embodied and enacted in a human life. The life of the incarnate one itself discloses the reality of God and embodies His creative will for man. Christ himself corresponds with these realities. Now language is certainly the basic medium of the conveyance of truth. But we have noted something of the difficulty, for limited human powers of expression, of bringing divine realities to expression in words. Hence, we may suppose, the revelatory power of the Word of God made flesh. We are not left alone to struggle with the gap between our words and the divine reality. God comes to meet us where we are in the incarnate Word. This is presumably what the author of the Fourth Gospel means us to understand by the words 'I am the truth', placed on the lips of Jesus, namely, that Jesus himself embodies and expresses both the truth about God and the truth about man as he was meant to be. This is the truth to which Jesus and the Spirit bear witness. It is this truth that will make men free.

The notion of truth which is not just expressed in words but embodied in human life is not peculiar to religion. A 'true friend' is a friend who embodies in life and in action the ideal reality of friendship. He corresponds with that ideal. We discover the truth about friendship from our dealings with him. In the context of Christian incarnational religion this usage becomes central. As Austin Farrer put the matter, with characteristic lucidity, 'Men may construct a myth expressive of divine truths as they conceive them, and the stuff of that myth will be words. God has constructed a myth expressive of the living truths he intends to convey, and the stuff of the myth is facts.' God's parable, on Farrer's view, is a real human life and death.[15]

When it is claimed in the Fourth Gospel that the truth will make men free, this is not to be understood in a gnostic sense, as if certain esoteric truths brought to our awareness had an automatic liberating effect. The truths in question are moral and spiritual truths of compelling practical significance. But again it is not a peculiar religious sense of 'truth' that has these practical implications. It is rather the realities disclosed in the words and works of Christ and in the Person of Christ himself that lay upon us these constraints to action.

It must be pointed out that even in these profoundly religious contexts of incarnate, moral and practical truth the same basic sense of 'truth' is still maintained – namely, that which expresses or shows how things are and were meant to be. Nor does any of this absolve us from attention to the second-order question of the truth of christological doctrine. The Christian Church may claim that Jesus is the truth. We have seen what that claim means. But the question remains, whether the claim is true.

12

Further reflections and responses

In the years since the original debate, one of the authors of
The Myth of God Incarnate has acknowledged that he has ceased
to believe in God and resigned his orders in the Church[1] and
another has gone on to develop an even more radical, purely
expressivist, conception of the Christian religion in which
'God' is held to be the name, not for an objective, personal,
source of all finite being and value, but rather for a projected
religious ideal by which we who call ourselves Christians may
hope to live.[2] It might well be thought that the debate about
the objective reality of God is much more central and much
more far-reaching than the christological debate about the
divinity of Jesus Christ, which clearly presupposes theism in
the strong sense of belief in an objective God. Yet, as I said
in the Preface to this collection, I remain convinced that the
christological debate is the more serious and central debate
for the continuing identity of Christianity. I would certainly
argue that Christianity, like many though not all other
religions, is committed to the reality of God; and the issue of
whether there is indeed an infinite personal ground of being
is a life or death issue for Christianity. Yet there is a sense in
which the special contribution of Christianity to world
religion only arises when that basic question has already been
settled in favour of theism. I cannot seriously believe that the
Christian Churches will ever concede the possibility that in
essence religion and especially Christianity are not concerned
with God in the objective sense. (Consequently it seems to me

to be much the more intelligible and proper course of action
for someone who has ceased to believe in an objective God,
if he is a priest, to resign his orders and to leave the Church.)

It is the internal, christological debate, presupposing belief
in God, between those who hold that Jesus Christ was and is
God made man and those who believe him to have been a,
perhaps the, chosen, spirit-filled yet purely human, representative of God to man, that is the crucial debate over what
precisely the specifically Christian religion is all about. Here,
as I said in the Preface, there is the genuine possibility of non-
incarnational Christology coming to prevail, at least in broad
sections of the Christian Church. I have noticed that, even
among critics of *The Myth of God Incarnate*, there is a surprising
tendency to concede too much to the authors of *The Myth* and
to defend the divinity of Christ in a somewhat watered-down,
usually functionalist, way – a way which blurs the distinc-
tiveness of the claim that Jesus Christ was and is God made
man, and which fails to explicate this claim in terms of a
strongly trinitarian doctrine of God. This fact only mirrors,
as it were, from this side of the 'Myth' watershed, the tendencies which I singled out for comment in chapter 1 above and
which can be seen as leading to their logical conclusion in
The Myth. Also relevant to consideration of the possibility of
non-incarnational Christologies coming to prevail is their
appearance now in Roman Catholic theology as well (see
chapter 7). But one of the things brought home to me by
discussion of the substance of chapter 6 in Germany in 1978
was the greater stress in German Protestant theology on the
doctrine of Redemption than on the doctrine of the Incarnation. Of course there are notable exceptions in the work of
Eberhard Jüngel and Jürgen Moltmann, to whom appeal was
made in chapter 4. But Wolfhart Pannenberg only retains
an incarnational Christology by the skin of his teeth in the
extremely difficult and roundabout conceptuality of *Jesus, God
and Man*,[3] and elsewhere an unwillingness to try to spell out

the ontological implications of Christian soteriology seems to prevail. So, it has to be admitted that there are signs, not only in Anglo-Saxon theology, but in Roman Catholic and German Protestant theology as well, of a loss of nerve in the exposition and defence of the doctrine of the divinity of Jesus Christ.

The essays collected together in this volume will have shown why I think it necessary to expound and defend that doctrine in a strong, objective and realist sense, as not only belonging to the essence of Christianity but also constituting its most special and significant truth. It remains in this new and final chapter to consider some of the criticisms of such a stance that have been made and to offer a few further reflections on the centrality of incarnational Christology.

One of the first critics of my stress on the uniqueness of the Incarnation was my friend and former colleague, Keith Ward.[4] His article suggested that the difference between incarnation and inspiration represented a false dichotomy. All we need for an adequate Christology is the belief that Jesus was 'a man in whom the glory of God was manifested fully, and through whom God will bring to himself all who will respond'. It is still unclear to me how a reduced 'functionalist' Christology can sustain the 'fully' in that quotation. But Ward supports his case by sharp criticism of three of my arguments for belief in a unique incarnation, that is, for belief in Jesus as God made man. In the first place, he points out, we ourselves, two thousand years later on, do *not* enjoy a face-to-face encounter with God in the man Jesus personally. Secondly, God must be thought to suffer with *all* who suffer, not just in Jesus. Thirdly, Ward throws out a number of supposed parallels designed to ridicule my suggestion that reduced claims for what God did in Christ fail, once we allow that God might have become man. It is not too difficult to rebut these criticisms. I admit that our personal commerce with God through Jesus Christ is different from an ordinary face-to-face human encounter. But I see no point in labouring the differences when it is agreed that it is our knowledge of *God* that is in question. The point to be stressed, surely, is that Christian knowledge of God consists in personal encounter with God in and through the spiritual and sacramental presence and activity of the one who lived and died a human life and death nearly two thousand years ago and whom we read about in the Gospels. There still seems to me to be all the difference in the world between the notion that a particular human being manifested certain general characteristics expressive of God's nature and the notion that God himself has come amongst us as a man and made his own humanity a permanent focus and channel of his self-giving love towards us.

Nor does the idea that God suffers with every sufferer, true though it is, have the same moral force as the idea that God *himself* suffered on the Cross. Sympathy is an admirable quality but it is no substitute for accepting responsibility for the world's ills by exposing oneself to them. Ward draws the alternatives quite falsely when he says, 'God must enter into the world's sorrow at every point, not just in one human life.' The point is that God not only enters into the world's sorrow at every point but also makes *himself* vulnerable to it by incarnation. It is the latter fact which demonstrates the truth of the former, and it is incarnation, not inspiration, that enables us to say this.

I see no point in generalising the form of my argument about the relative weakness of reduced claims for what God has done in Christ. I was urging the great moral force of the doctrine of the Incarnation. That presupposed its making sense. If sense is conceded, my point about the weaker force of reduced claims surely stands.

I must admit to some surprise and disappointment on reading Ward's rejoinder. I greatly admire his work in the philosophy of religion and find myself in almost complete agreement with his rational theology. But I find a lack of sensitivity and control in his writing on doctrinal theology. His popular book, *The Living God*,[5] illustrates this problem. Metaphysically persuasive, it fails to convince theologically. The point of the Christian doctrines of the Trinity and Incarnation seems to escape him. This was already clear at the end of the above-mentioned article, where we find him introducing the gratuitous notion of 'a totally unique species of being' to characterise what he takes to be the Chalcedonian conception of one who is truly God and truly man. But the doctrine of the Incarnation has never involved such a *tertium quid*. Jesus was certainly a member of the species *homo sapiens*. But God is in no genus or species. His transcendent Being, Christians believe, is such as to be able, without loss of transcendence or indeed of universal immanence, to include being made man – and of course that means a real man with a particular history and social context behind and around him.

This point, so well understood by Austin Farrer,[6] seems beyond the capacity of many contemporary philosophical theologians to grasp. I have pointed out in an earlier chapter[7] how Don Cupitt trades on excessively anthropomorphic images of God in order to criticise the doctrine of the Incarnation. Sadly, I observe the same fault in a major book by David Brown,[8] which otherwise offers a resolute defence of the doctrines of the Incarnation and the Trinity. The very same reason – an over-literal anthropomorphic concept of God – leads Brown to echo the authors of *The Myth* in accusing many defenders of orthodoxy of incoherence, to drive a wedge between Chalcedonian and kenotic models of the Incarnation (picturing the latter on the analogy of reincarnation), and to defend a relational conception of the Trinity by the most inappropriate appeal to the analogy of schizophrenia.

Before returning to criticisms of my own contributions to the debate, I should like to comment on a more recent survey of the issues by the late John Robinson.[9] I have already mentioned Robinson's Hulsean Lectures as one of the indications of the trend leading in the direction of *The Myth*.[10] In his more recent essay, commenting on the whole 'Myth' debate, Robinson tries to distance himself from both sides and to defend something of a cross-bench view. He certainly wanted – against *The Myth* authors – to maintain the uniqueness of Christ and of what God did in him. For Robinson, the key verse of scripture is 2 Corinthians 5.19: 'God was in Christ reconciling the world to himself.' But that verse is ambiguous. It is susceptible both of a functionalist and of an incarnational interpretation. I have defended the incarnational interpretation: God was in Christ, in the sense of substantial presence in person, himself acting out a human life and death. Robinson clearly wished to maintain a functionalist interpretation: God was in Christ, in the sense of acting in and through this man for the world's salvation. Jesus was God's unique representative. But on my view that is the first step on the slippery slope that leads to *The Myth*.

In fact Robinson tries to have it both ways, but only succeeds in muddying the waters by virtually misquoting Farrer: 'Christ is not just a man doing human things divinely, like any saint or seer, but a man doing divine things humanly.'[11] Farrer, however, wrote, 'a good man helped by Grace may do human things divinely, Christ did divine things humanly.'[12] Farrer's formulation does not involve a denial that Christ was a man, but clearly, for Farrer, in the Incarnation the humanity was adjectival upon the divinity. Christ is primarily a divine subject. The man is the vehicle not just of divine action in the world, but of divine substantial and particular presence in the world. He is Emmanuel – God with us. In that sense, his acts are God's acts. Robinson's formulation, by contrast, makes little sense. The difference between doing human things divinely and doing divine things humanly is highly obscure when it is insisted that the subject in each case is a man and no more.

159

Robinson wants to maintain the doctrine of the Incarnation, but fights shy of the idea that what is embodied in Jesus is a personal centre or subjectivity within the Godhead. Rather it is God's creative self-expressive activity that is embodied in Jesus. Despite the fact that this is offered as a gloss on the incarnation of the *Word*, it is clear that, for Robinson, the Word has lost the substantial meaning that it had in classical trinitarian doctrine. Clearly we are on the road which leads to the unitarian views of Lampe and Wiles.[13] Again we see how the doctrines of the Incarnation and the Trinity go together.

In returning to criticisms of my own work, I now take up the important issue of religious pluralism. As I have conceded in several of the pieces assembled in this volume, the most powerful argument against traditional incarnational Christology comes out of the encounter of religions; for it is very hard to do justice to the spirituality and religious worth of the great world religions and at the same time to maintain the divinity and hence finality of Christ. In a useful study of this problem,[14] Alan Race has distinguished three main types of current Christian theology of religion and the religions – exclusivism (typified by Karl Barth), inclusivism (typified by Karl Rahner), and pluralism (typified by John Hick). In endorsing the last of these, Race was bound to follow the path of the authors of *The Myth* in trying to demythologise the doctrine of the Incarnation. It is interesting to observe that he too recognises that a functionalist, 'degree', Christology (such as that espoused by Robinson) cannot really sustain an 'inclusivist' position still giving Christ a final, 'decisive', status *vis-à-vis* the ultimate salvation of all men. Race consistently opts for the more radical pluralist position. But his criticism of the traditional incarnational Christology is weak. He sees it as involving divine intervention from outside, failing entirely to appreciate that God's own personal self-presentation in Jesus Christ takes *immanence* to its furthest point – not just universal presence within the created world, but particular presence in person. There immanence is focused in an individual who actually *is* the divine Son. At the same time creation at its highest point – humanity – is taken into God, when a particular human individual lives out God's own life on earth.

Race also has problems with the concept of pre-existence, taking it to contradict full humanity. But, as I argue in chapter 6, it is not the man Jesus who 'pre-existed', but God the Son. And it is precisely the doctrine of the Incarnation that attributes 'full humanity', that is, the full humanity of Jesus, to God the Son in his incarnate state, not only two thousand years ago but from then on in all eternity. For although the human Jesus did not 'pre-exist', the risen Lord exists for ever in God, as God's permanent 'human face'.

Criticising my own contribution, Race does little more than echo Ward's points, which I have already dealt with above. I still think personal encounter with God in Christ and God's taking suffering on *himself* in the Cross are two key elements lost when incarnational Christology is abandoned. (I also think that the loss of trinitarian belief and of conviction of Christ's living spiritual and sacramental presence and of the eschatological dimension of Christ's lordship – these are not mentioned by Race – are major deprivations in a pluralist solution to the problem of the religions.) Finally Race again quotes Ward's rejection of the 'substance' terminology implied by my defence of incarnational Christology. This is a red herring. Ontology – 'substance' talk – is involved in any serious theistic belief. Whether we speak of God's action in the man Jesus or of God's personal presence *as* the man Jesus, we are using the category of substance. What is at issue is the manner of God's presence. I maintain that Christianity is to be identified by its special understanding of the revelatory and salvific significance of God's presence in person in and as the man Jesus.

So, on my view, pluralism only escapes the dilemma of Christianity and the world religions by abandoning what is most distinctive and special about Christianity. I have no desire to maintain exclusivism. I hold the most promising approach to be that of inclusivism, and, as I say, that requires incarnational ontology to make sense of the idea of the universal presence and activity not just of God but of Christ.[15]

I turn to the most interesting criticism of my contribution to the 'Myth' debate, that of Geoffrey Lampe in a review of the Birmingham colloquy.[16] Lampe's first point is that the question is begged by the equation of the divinity of Christ with 'the particular interpretation of Christ's divinity adopted by the incarnational clauses of the classical creeds'. Well, certainly I hold that the Church is committed to the divinity of Christ as summarised in the incarnational clauses of the Apostles' and the Nicene creeds. They hardly seem to me to constitute *interpretations*. The Athanasian creed is quite different. Here we are indeed in the realm of interpretation and there is no reason to suppose that we are tied down to the detailed theology, still less the terminology, of the Athanasian creed. Lampe points out correctly that my own rejection of divine passibility and defence of kenosis are far removed from Patristic Christology. But divine impassibility and Chalcedonian terminology are not themselves embedded in the Apostles' or the Nicene creed. Lampe makes the further point, echoing Cupitt, that it is not clear why 'Hebblethwaite's divergencies from tradition are legitimate whereas to question the credal formulation of the doctrines of the Incarnation and the Trinity is not'. In fact I do not wish to tie us down to particular credal formulations; but it is surely not implausible to suggest that while the doctrines of the Incarnation and the Trinity are of the essence of Christianity and thus indispensable, various interpretations *of those doctrines* are permissible. Chalcedonian and kenotic Christologies are, I submit, different interpretations of those doctrines (and not

necessarily exclusive ones, as David Brown maintains). But in
the end I can only submit my own sense of what is illegitimate
and what is legitimate to the judgement of my fellow
Christians.

I agree that the best way to resolve these matters is to produce superior theological arguments. But I still think that the
Church, through the bishops, or even through the General
Synod, has the right to repudiate heterodox views, in particular to keep them out of the liturgies and any official doctrinal statements of the faith of the Church.

Lampe proceeds to some more detailed criticisms of my
contributions to the 'Myth' debate. Against my formulation
that 'we predicate divinity of Jesus because we believe the
humanity to be the vehicle and expression of the eternal Son',
he set his own preferred version: 'we predicate divinity of
Jesus because we believe him to be the vehicle and expression
of the eternal God'. The ease with which Lampe converts
what was intended as an expression of incarnational
Christology into what can be taken in a non-incarnational
sense shows how difficult it is to get these formulations right.
I would resist replacement of 'the eternal Son' by 'God'
simpliciter just because I think the trinitarian doctrine alone
enables us to speak in a serious sense of the divinity of Jesus
Christ. That human life – and I certainly do not mean
'impersonal humanity' – was lived out from a centre in God
and the relation of Jesus to the Father manifests in
human–divine terms the internal relations within the
Godhead. Lampe's formulation could still mean all this, but
it is clear that he himself wants it to be interpreted non-
incarnationally. But on that interpretation, predicating *divinity* of Jesus Christ makes very little sense, and I still fail to see
how such a functionalist reading provides an adequate
account of the unique perfection and continuing import of
Jesus. It seems to me that Lampe is trading on traditional-
sounding language while offering an interpretation that fails

to do the traditional job. Not surprisingly, a number of the authors of *The Myth* go further and deny uniqueness, sinlessness and finality to Jesus.

Lampe's relentless criticism next takes up another formulation of mine. In trying to expound a kenotic view, I said, 'God *qua* God is aware of who he is . . . but *qua* man (i.e. as Jesus) his self-awareness is limited to a filial sense of dependence on the Father. For this reason incarnational Christology attributes two consciousnesses, not to Jesus, but to God incarnate'. Lampe comments that, on this formulation, 'the *communicatio idiomatum* seems to have become a one-way process. The ancients would surely have preferred to say that, in his divine nature, Jesus who is God incarnate is aware of who he is, and, in his human nature, the self-awareness of Jesus who is God incarnate is limited – and granted their presuppositions, their formulation seems clearer than Hebblethwaite's.' The *communicatio idiomatum* is an ancient doctrine whereby the predicates appropriate to divinity and humanity may be properly applied to each nature in the hypostatic union which constitutes the Incarnation. It is a good example of an ancient formulation to which we need not feel committed; but something of its force can be maintained if we insist that, while the humanity is indeed taken into God, the divine attributes must take an appropriate human form when predicated of the incarnate one, *qua* man. Thus the man Jesus was not omniscient, but he knew what was in the heart of man. Similarly the divine omnipotence was made known in the weakness of the man on the Cross and was exemplified in the self-limitation. Thus, on a kenotic view, the *communicatio idiomatum* is not a one-way process, but the human expression of divine attributes requires self-limitation in a way in which the divine awareness of the human experience does not. Nor am I persuaded that the Fathers' way of putting things, as Lampe summarises it, is actually clearer than mine. For it does not bring out the fact that, on an incarnational view, the primary subject of the

incarnate life is God in one of the modes of his trinitarian
being. Nor does it really make much sense to attribute two
consciousnesses to *Jesus*. That is why the kenotic view is to be
preferred.

Lampe's reply to my argument that without the trinitarian
doctrine creation must be necessary to God if he is to enjoy the
fullness of being as love is most unsatisfactory. Lampe asserts
that 'it is of the nature of God, being love, to create and to participate in the reciprocities of his creatures; there is no need to
postulate a reciprocity of persons within the Godhead'. My
point about God's being love, on this view, being *dependent* on
creation surely stands. Certainly it is of God's nature to participate in the reciprocities of his creatures, but only because he
is in himself love given and received.

Finally Lampe 'wants to ask Hebblethwaite why his admirable perception that man's response to God is made "in
God" seems to him to imply an incarnational rather than
. . . an inspirational Christology, and why, unless on the basis
of an extremely anthropomorphic idea of God, he insists
against Hick that only one man in all history can actually be
God.' The answer to the first of these two questions is that
Lampe has totally misconstrued my point about man's
response to God. That was not a christological point at all.
It concerned the doctrine of the Spirit, not the Incarnation.
Admittedly, I did suggest that experience of the Spirit
discloses another God–God relation within the Trinity, but
that has nothing whatsoever to do with the doctrine of the
Incarnation (except that, of course, the man Jesus was, like
us, *also* and, indeed, supremely inspired by the Spirit).

The second question is much more pertinent. It is raised
by Cupitt and Race as well as by Hick and Lampe, and
clearly reveals a point of deep incomprehension in critics of
the doctrine of the Incarnation about its full significance in the
Christian tradition. The suggestion that God, in the Person
of his Son, might become incarnate in more than one human

being is to operate with a totally different idea of incarnation from that informing the Christian tradition. For that tradition, God the Son's coming amongst us as one of us is necessarily particular and unique, because the whole history of the world from start to finish is there seen as pivoted upon *that* personal self-identification of Creator and creation. Consider the eschatological implications of pluralism in the sense of many incarnations. If God's personal commerce with mankind is channelled for ever through a variety of mediators, the ultimate consummation is bound to be diverse rather than one. Christian tradition, by contrast, has offered a unitary conception of revelation, redemption and consummation. This is not, as Lampe suggests, a consequence of an anthropomorphic idea of God. It is a consequence of a unitary idea of God and human destiny. A God who is both transcendent and immanent, omnipresent and personal, one and three, is not an anthropomorphic God. But out of his great love this God, who in himself remains beyond our comprehension, anthropomorphises himself, identifies himself, without ceasing to be the triune God, with his creation in the individual man, Jesus, towards whom all history was leading, in relation to whom all subsequent history takes its meaning, and in whom all things will in the end be summed up in God. This individual himself, then, has to be thought of in universal terms as the cosmic Logos behind all other partial revelations of God. But when God's work is complete, it is Christ who will be seen by all to be the head of creation, *the* human face of God for all men and women for all eternity. As such, the incarnate Son can of course only be thought of as one.

Another criticism of my argument against the possibility of multiple incarnations is to be found in T. V. Morris' book, *The Logic of God Incarnate.*[17] This is all the more strange in that it comes in the context of a resolute defence of the coherence of the traditional orthodox doctrine. The reason why Morris wishes to defend the possibility of multiple incar-

166

nations is to allow for the possibility of other incarnations of God the Son among extraterrestrials on other planets if such there be. But the logic of his argument permits the *possibility* of other incarnations here on earth, even if there have in fact not been any. Morris finds my rejection of this notion surprising, since he thinks that my defence of some sort of two-consciousnesses or two-minds view of the incarnate Son allows for the possibility of multiple incarnations. The idea that an earthly range of consciousness can be contained in, without containing, the divine range of consciousness, in Morris' opinion, in no way restricts this relation to a single finite, range of consciousness. 'There could be only one person involved in all these incarnations – God the Son – but this one person could be incarnate in any number of created bodies and minds, such as the body and earthly mind of Jesus.'[18] I am not persuaded that Morris does justice here to what a full doctrine of divine incarnation entails. It is not only a matter of Jesus' mind and will expressing the mind and will of God here on earth in our midst. The whole person of Jesus, his unique character and personality express God to us; for he is God the Son in person. As I have been arguing all along, the idea of many human individuals incarnating God the Son introduces a deep incoherence into the notion of what it is to be a person; it undervalues the seriousness of the idea that a unique human personality is here expressing in life and in act who and what God is, and, as emphasised in the previous paragraph, it has completely unacceptable consequences for eschatology.

It is also odd to find Morris conceding that God the Son may *in fact* have become incarnate only once, despite the *possibility* of multiple incarnations here on earth. It certainly would involve no modal fallacy[19] in this context to press Wiles' objection that God could be accused of parsimoniousness if he failed to avail himself of other opportunities to come to the rescue of segments of the human race. On the traditional view there *must* be a morally sufficient reason behind the *de facto* uniqueness of the Incarnation. The clearest reason would be the fact, if it is a fact, that incarnation in the fullest sense is *logically* possible only once. Put in its strongest form, my argument would be that, once the nature of the Incarnation is understood in its fullest sense, it will be seen that the impossibility of multiple incarnations is a logical one.

My own discussion of the notion of multiple incarnations was restricted to the earth and human history. Morris, as I say, concerns himself primarily with the possibility of multiple incarnations among extraterrestrials on other planets. There has indeed been much talk of this possibility, not only by atheistic minds, for whom the capacity of matter so to combine as to produce intelligent life is a general (though inexplicable) fact, and, if it has happened here, it is likely to have happened elsewhere in the universe. Christians too have speculated along these lines, notably C. S. Lewis in the novel *Perelandra*,[20] where the first intelligent creatures on another planet are on the point of repeating the story of the Fall. Lewis speculates on the possibility of another incarnation of God the Son in *their* form to bring about *their* redemption. This of course would relativise the incarnation of God the Son in Jesus Christ to this planet and to human destiny. On my view that too would lead to eschatological incoherence, with a plurality of incarnations manifesting the one God to a diversity of personal creatures. I suggest that it is an implication of the Christian doctrine of the Incarnation, properly understood, that there are no other intelligent, personal creatures in God's creation than human beings here on earth. I am inclined to think that modern cosmology supports this view anyway and that general statistical arguments for extraterrestrial intelligence are a form of modern superstition.[21] For one thing it has been shown that the size and density of the universe has to be what it is, if life is to appear at all, and as far as we can tell, cosmic evolution in the direction

168

of complex living organisms here on earth requires more than chance interaction to be at all plausible. There are too many coincidences required at each stage of the whole process. Consequently, the theist will postulate an immanent principle, the divine Spirit, guiding cosmic evolution in such a way as to come up with life, intelligence and personhood, uniquely here on Earth. Such a scenario might well be thought to make better sense of incarnational Christology, with all its cosmic and eschatological ramifications. Admittedly this is highly speculative; but Karl Popper encourages us to produce falsifiable hypotheses. I submit this as a hypothesis, inviting, be it noted, empirical falsification.

I now turn to an objection raised not by radical but by conservative theologians. Not surprisingly, Eric Mascall liked my presentation of the doctrine of the Incarnation in the thought of Austin Farrer.[22] But he does take exception to my reservations about Farrer's 'residual subordinationism'.[23] The point was that, for Farrer, Jesus' dependence on the Father reflected the eternal derivedness or filiation in the Trinity; whereas, for me, it is solely a feature of the incarnate state, and need not be transferred to the Trinity as such. This is a somewhat esoteric dispute which hardly needs to be pressed especially when we read that, for Mascall, derivedness does not necessarily imply subordination and that 'derived equality' is a perfectly coherent concept.[24] Since my argument was against subordinationism, I can concede Mascall's point here, though it still seems reasonable to suggest that the manifest subordinationism of *Jesus'* relation to the Father is an aspect of the incarnate state rather than a reflection of the eternal derivation of the Son.

Mascall's criticism is echoed, without argument, by Michael Wilson in a footnote to an article on Farrer's Christology.[25] But Wilson also makes a much more serious point against me by questioning Farrer's commitment to the absolute difference between inspiration and incarnation. 'I suggest', writes Wilson, 'that the difference is radical but not complete. We must cling to the common factor, the Holy Spirit, who indwells and inspires Jesus and the Christian alike. The uniqueness that Farrer is claiming lies in the total-ity of the interpenetration of human and divine.' And he quotes Farrer from *Saving Belief*: 'In the person of Christ the mutual interpenetration is complete: it is necessary to talk of a personal identity.' This passage in Wilson's article strikes me as disastrous. It confuses utterly the roles of the persons of the Trinity in the Incarnation. The incarnate Son, *qua* man, was of course, like us, inspired by the Spirit – supremely so. But that was not what constituted incarnation. The complete interpenetration constituting incarnation was not the Spirit's, but the Son's presence on earth *as* a man. Farrer himself was quite clear about this.

In conclusion, I want to offer some further reflections on this basic difference between inspiration and incarnation. My conviction that liberals, modernists and radicals are all in danger of overlooking Christianity's special contribution to the history of religions – or at least of overlooking what makes sense of that special contribution (for despite their defective theology they remain disciples of Christ) – rests on perception of this difference. I find myself unable to concede that what I call a strong doctrine of the Incarnation is only one among a variety of equally plausible interpretations of the figure of Jesus Christ. On the contrary, what the early Chris-tians came to realise (and to interpret in various ways) was the fact that the God whom all men knew inarticulately as the source of their very being and who had revealed his nature and will through the prophets and sages of Israel had now identified himself with his Creation in an utterly unique and final way by coming amongst them as a man. We ourselves, without denying the special providential role of Israel and its prophets in preparing for the Incarnation, can extend this insight into God's preparatory work to the whole history of religions. But the same basic difference remains between inspired recognition of the existence, character and will of God on the one hand and personal encounter with God made man, living out and acting out his boundless love to the point of self-sacrificial death, on the other.

Moreover, once the divinity of Christ, in this substantial sense, is recognised, the whole story of God's commerce with his Creation, from start to finish, has to be rethought and retold. Christianity involves, as I have put it more than once, seeing that story as *pivoted* around the Incarnation. The God–world story leads up to God's incarnation – such a divine identification with and presence to the created universe having been intended from the start – and it continues in a radically different way from then on, in that from the moment of incarnation humanity exists for ever in God and the history of the world becomes the history of mankind's vocation to, and partial experience of, a share, by adoption, in Christ's Sonship. This phase in God's creative process only *begins* here on earth. Each person who dies, so Christians believe, is raised by God into further phases of the redemptive process and gradually united with God in Christ – though still, it must be added, in a way which differs from God's own incarnation in Christ himself.

Of course this is a rather one-sided way of characterising the post-Incarnation phase of God's creative process. A great deal else has happened and happens here on earth. The ethical significance of the Incarnation for life on earth is very great and very important. But man's whole existence and history throughout his manifold pursuit of the good (and failure to attain it) are ultimately determined, so Christians believe, by their final goal and intended consummation, when the perfected creation will be gathered up, through Christ, in God.

I get the impression that some theologians today do little more than add to a basically religious view of the world –

and sometimes, one has to say, to a basically secular view of the world – a sense of the great moral and spiritual worth of the example and teaching of Jesus. Sometimes this involves belief in life after death as well; but increasingly, it seems, even many Christians have lost confidence in that key aspect of the tradition. One realises that the difference between inspirational and incarnational Christology does not come out only in the intricacies of technical theology. It affects one's whole view of the world and one's readiness to think through the God–world relation, including its hoped-for eschatological resolution, in the light of the life, death and resurrection of Jesus Christ, understood as the life, death and resurrection of God incarnate.

Notes

1 INCARNATION – THE ESSENCE OF CHRISTIANITY?

1. N. Pittenger, *Christology Reconsidered* (SCM 1970); J. A. T. Robinson, *The Human Face of God* (SCM 1973); M. Wiles, *The Remaking of Christian Doctrine* (SCM 1974); J. Hick, *God and the Universe of Faiths* (Macmillan 1973); D. Cupitt, *The Leap of Reason* (Sheldon 1976).
2. N. Smart, 'Gods, Bliss and Morality', in *Christian Ethics and Contemporary Philosophy*, ed. I. T. Ramsey (SCM 1966), p. 25n. The danger in Christology of assuming a particular (and univocal) sense of 'place' is well brought out by T. F. Torrance in *Space, Time and Incarnation* (OUP 1969).
3. See G. Parrinder, *Avatar and Incarnation* (Faber 1970).

2 PERICHORESIS – REFLECTIONS ON THE DOCTRINE OF THE TRINITY

1. G. L. Prestige, *God in Patristic Thought* (2nd ed. SPCK 1952), p. 299.
2. The Doctrine Commission of the Church of England, *Christian Believing* (SPCK 1976), p. 126.
3. P. T. Geach, *God and the Soul* (RKP 1969), p. 109.
4. J. Calvin, *Institutes of the Christian Religion*, Bk I, ch. XIII.
5. E. Troeltsch, *Christian Thought* (ULP 1923), p. 32.
6. L. Hodgson, *The Doctrine of the Trinity* (Nisbet 1943), p. 32.
7. M. Wiles, *Working Papers in Doctrine* (SCM 1976), ch. I.
8. A. Farrer, *Saving Belief* (Hodder 1964), p. 128.
9. G. W. H. Lampe, *God as Spirit* (OUP 1977).
10. H. Williams, 'Incarnation: Model and Symbol', *Theology*, January 1976.

4 THE MORAL AND RELIGIOUS VALUE OF THE
INCARNATION

1 A. Farrer, 'Very God and Very Man', in *Interpretation and Belief*, ed. C. Conti (SPCK 1976), p. 128.
2 N. Smart, *A Dialogue of Religions* (SCM 1960), chs. VI and VII. This book was republished as a Pelican paperback under the title *World Religions: A Dialogue.*
3 J. Hick (ed.), *The Myth of God Incarnate* (SCM 1976), p. 80.
4 *Ibid.*, p. 141.
5 John 13.1.
6 J. Hick, *God and the Universe of Faiths* (Fount Paperback Edition, Collins 1977), p. xvii.
7 P. T. Geach, *Providence and Evil* (CUP 1977), pp. 24–8.
8 D. Cupitt, 'Jesus and the Meaning of God', in *Incarnation and Myth: The Debate Continued*, ed. M. Goulder (SCM Press 1979), p. 40.
9 L. Houlden, 'The Creed of Experience', in *The Myth*, pp. 131f.
10 *Incarnation and Myth*, pp. 78f.
11 *The Myth*, p. 30.
12 *Ibid.*, p. 202.
13 *God as Spirit*, p. 111.
14 *Ibid.*, p. 139.
15 *God and the Universe of Faiths*, pp. 69f.
16 G. K. A. Bell and A. Deissmann (eds.), *Mysterium Christi* (Longmans 1930), pp. 167–90.
17 A. Farrer, *Saving Belief*, p. 99.
18 H. U. von Balthasar, *Love Alone: The Way of Revelation* (Burns and Oates 1968), p. 120.
19 *Ibid.*, p. 71.
20 *Ibid.*, p. 66.
21 T. F. Torrance, *God and Rationality* (OUP 1971), p. 137.
22 J. Moltmann, *The Crucified God* (SCM Press 1974), p. 215.
23 *Ibid.*, p. 255.
24 E. Jüngel, *God as the Mystery of the World* (T. & T. Clark 1983), pp. 316ff.

5 FURTHER REMARKS ON THE 'MYTH' DEBATE

1 *Incarnation and Myth*, p. 45.
2 *Ibid.*, p. 55.
3 I. T. Ramsey, *Christian Empiricism* (Sheldon 1974), pp. 98ff.

[4] Thomas Aquinas, *Summa Theologiae*, 1a 13, art. 6.
[5] See chapter 1 above.
[6] *The Myth*, p. 11.

6 THE PROPRIETY OF THE DOCTRINE OF THE INCARNATION AS A WAY OF INTERPRETING CHRIST

[1] C. Gore (ed.), *Lux Mundi* (John Murray 1890).
[2] C. Gore, *The Incarnation of the Son of God* (John Murray 1891).
[3] H. P. Liddon, *The Divinity of Our Lord and Saviour Jesus Christ* (Longmans 1867).
[4] C. Gore, *Dissertations on Subjects Connected with the Incarnation* (John Murray 1895).
[5] J. R. Illingworth, *Personality Human and Divine* (Macmillan 1894). See also *Lux Mundi*.
[6] J. Macquarrie, *Twentieth Century Religious Thought* (SCM Press 1963), p. 39.
[7] R. C. Moberly, *Atonement and Personality* (John Murray 1901). See also *Lux Mundi* and *Foundations* (note 11).
[8] W. Sanday, *Christologies Ancient and Modern* (OUP 1910). See also Sanday and N. P. Williams, *Form and Content in the Christian Tradition* (Longmans 1916).
[9] F. Weston, *The One Christ* (Longmans 1907).
[10] H. M. Relton, *A Study in Christology* (SPCK 1917).
[11] B. H. Streeter (ed.), *Foundations* (Macmillan 1912).
[12] W. Temple (ed.), *Christus Veritas* (Macmillan 1924).
[13] G. K. A. Bell and A. Deissmann (eds.), *Mysterium Christi* (Longmans 1928).
[14] L. S. Thornton, *The Incarnate Lord* (Longmans 1928).
[15] L. W. Grensted, *The Person of Christ* (Nisbet 1933).
[16] H. Rashdall, *The Idea of Atonement in Christian Theology* (Macmillan 1919). See also Rashdall *et al.*, *Contentio Veritatis* (John Murray 1902) and 'The Modern Churchman', 1921.
[17] J. F. Bethune-Baker, *The Miracle of Christianity* (Longmans 1914); *The Faith of the Apostles' Creed* (Macmillan 1918); 'The Modern Churchman', 1921.
[18] E. G. Selwyn (ed.), *Essays Catholic and Critical* (SPCK 1926).
[19] J. K. Mozley, *The Doctrine of the Incarnation* (Bles 1936).
[20] O. C. Quick, *Modern Philosophy and the Incarnation* (SPCK 1915); *Essays in Orthodoxy* (Macmillan 1916); *Liberalism, Modernism and Tradition* (Longmans 1922); *Christian Beliefs and Modern Questions*

(SCM 1923); *The Ground of Faith and the Chaos of Thought* (Nisbet 1931); *The Gospel of Divine Action* (Dutton 1933); *Doctrines of the Creed* (Nisbet 1938).

21 SPCK 1938 (reprinted, with a new introduction by G. W. H. Lampe, SPCK 1982).

22 J. M. Creed, *The Divinity of Jesus Christ* (CUP 1938).

23 A. E. J. Rawlinson (ed.), *Essays on the Trinity and the Incarnation* (Longmans 1933).

24 L. Hodgson, *And Was Made Man* (Longmans 1928); *The Doctrine of the Trinity* (Nisbet 1943); *The Doctrine of the Atonement* (Nisbet 1951); *Theology and the Gospel of Christ* (SPCK 1977).

25 W. R. Matthews, *The Problem of Christ in the Twentieth Century* (OUP 1950).

26 E. L. Mascall, *Christ, the Christian and the Church* (Longmans 1946); *Theology and the Gospel of Christ* (SPCK 1977).

27 A. M. Farrer, *Saving Belief* (Hodder 1964); *Interpretation and Belief* (SPCK 1976).

28 See chapter 9 below.

29 J. Macquarrie, *Principles of Christian Theology* (SCM 1966).

30 D. M. Baillie, *God Was In Christ* (Scribners 1948).

31 A. R. Vidler (ed.), *Soundings* (CUP 1962); N. Pittenger (ed.), *Christ For Us Today* (SCM 1968).

32 J. A. T. Robinson, *The Human Face of God* (SCM 1973). See also S. W. Sykes and J. P. Clayton (eds.), *Christ, Faith and History* (CUP 1972).

33 M. F. Wiles, *The Remaking of Christian Doctrine* (SCM 1974); *Working Papers in Doctrine* (SCM 1976).

34 G. W. H. Lampe, *God as Spirit* (OUP 1977). See also *Soundings*, *Christ For Us Today* and *Christ, Faith and History*.

35 For studies of Anglican Christology, see L. S. Lawton, *Conflict in Christology: A Study of British and American Christology from 1889–1914* (SPCK 1947); J. K. Mozley, *Some Tendencies in British Theology (from the Publication of Lux Mundi to the Present Day)* (SPCK 1951); L. B. Smedes, *The Incarnation: Trends in Anglican Thought* (Amsterdam 1953); A. M. Ramsey, *From Gore to Temple: The Development of Anglican Theology between Lux Mundi and the Second World War* (Longmans 1960).

36 See chapter 1 above.

37 A. M. Farrer, *The Brink of Mystery* (SPCK 1976), p. 19. See also chapter 9 below.

38 Farrer, *A Celebration of Faith* (Hodder 1970), p. 89.

39 Farrer, *Interpretation and Belief* (SPCK 1976), p. 135.
40 W. Temple, *Christus Veritas* (Macmillan 1924), p. 142.
41 D. M. MacKinnon, 'The Relation of the Doctrines of the Incarnation and the Trinity', in R. McKinney (ed.), *Creation, Christ and Culture* (T. & T. Clark 1976); see also *Christ, Faith and History*. G. C. Stead, *Divine Substance* (OUP 1977).
42 A. E. J. Rawlinson, *The New Testament Doctrine of Christ* (Longmans 1929).
43 E. Hoskyns and N. Davey, *The Riddle of the New Testament* (Faber 1931).
44 C. F. D. Moule, *The Origin of Christology* (CUP 1977).
45 O. C. Quick, *Doctrines of the Creed* (Nisbet 1938), ch. XIV.

7 THE CHURCH AND CHRISTOLOGY

1 M. Wiles, *The Remaking of Christian Doctrine* (SCM 1974), *passim*.
2 See note 45 to chapter 6 above.
3 See chapter 6 above.
4 K. Barth, *Church Dogmatics* (E. T., T. & T. Clark 1936–69).
5 *Time Magazine*, February 1978.
6 See his article in Hebblethwaite and Sutherland (eds.), *The Philosophical Frontiers of Christian Theology* (CUP 1982).
7 Anglican–Roman Catholic International Commission, *The Final Report* (CTS/SPCK 1982).
8 H. Küng, *On Being a Christian* (E. T., Collins 1977).
9 E. Schillebeeckx, *Jesus, an Experiment in Christology* (E. T., Collins 1979).
10 E. Schillebeeckx, *Christ, the Christian Experience in the Modern World* (SCM Press 1980).
11 E. Schillebeeckx, *Interim Report on the Books Jesus and Christ* (SCM Press 1980).
12 P. Hebblethwaite, *The New Inquisition?* (Collins 1980).
13 J. A. T. Robinson, *Honest to God* (SCM Press 1962).
14 The relevant correspondence is to be found in *Karl Barth–Rudolf Bultmann, Briefwechsel 1922–1966* (Theologischer Verlag Zürich 1971).
15 S. W. Sykes, *The Integrity of Anglicanism* (Mowbrays 1978).

8 CHRIST TODAY AND TOMORROW

1 The Doctrine Commission of the Church of England, *Christian Believing* (SPCK 1976).

2 D. Cupitt, *Taking Leave of God* (SCM Press 1980).
3 J. Moltmann, *The Trinity and the Kingdom of God* (E. T., SCM Press 1981).
4 G. Downing, *Has Christianity a Revelation?* (SCM Press 1964).
5 W. Pannenberg, *Basic Questions in Theology*, vol. 2 (E. T., SCM Press 1971).
6 See chapter 6, note 45.
7 J. Hick, *God Has Many Names* (Macmillan 1980).
8 P. Tillich, 'The Significance of the History of Religions for Systematic Theology', in J. C. Brauer (ed.), *The Future of Religions* (Chicago University Press 1966).

9 THE DOCTRINE OF THE INCARNATION IN THE THOUGHT OF AUSTIN FARRER

1 *Said or Sung* (Faith Press 1960); *A Celebration of Faith* (Hodder 1970); *The End of Man* (SPCK 1973); *The Brink of Mystery* (SPCK 1976).
2 SPCK 1976.
3 Hodder 1964.
4 A. Farrer, *Love Almighty and Ills Unlimited* (Collins 1962), ch. 7.
5 *Interpretation and Belief*, p. 128.
6 See Farrer's essay on 'Revelation' in B. Mitchell (ed.), *Faith and Logic* (George Allen and Unwin 1957), p. 98.
7 A. Farrer, *finite and Infinite* (Dacre Press 1943), p. 300.
8 A. Farrer, *The Glass of Vision* (Dacre Press 1948), p. 37.
9 *Saving Belief*, pp. 111–12.
10 *Interpretation and Belief*, p. 128.
11 A. Farrer, *A Science of God?*, pp. 121–2.
12 *A Celebration of Faith*, p. 88.
13 *Saving Belief*, p. 99.
14 *A Science of God?*, p. 127.
15 *The Glass of Vision*, p. 39.
16 *Interpretation and Belief*, p. 128.
17 *The Brink of Mystery*, p. 19.
18 *Faith and Logic*, p. 98.
19 *The Glass of Vision*, p. 40.
20 *A Celebration of Faith*, p. 88.
21 *Saving Belief*, p. 128.
22 *Interpretation and Belief*, p. 131.
23 A. Farrer, *Lord, I Believe*, p. 39.

24 *The Brink of Mystery*, p. 20.
25 L. Hodgson, *The Doctrine of the Trinity* (Nisbet 1943).
26 *Ibid.*
27 *Interpretation and Belief*, p. 130.
28 *Saving Belief*, p. 69.
29 *A Celebration of Faith*, p. 89.
30 *Ibid.*
31 *Saving Belief*, p. 157.
32 *Love Almighty and Ills Unlimited*, p. 129.
33 *The Brink of Mystery*, p. 20.
34 A. Farrer, *Faith and Speculation* (A. & C. Black 1967), p. 103.
35 *Saving Belief*, pp. 70–1.
36 *Interpretation and Belief*, p. 135.
37 *Saving Belief*, p. 75.
38 *Ibid.*, p. 125.
39 *Interpretation and Belief*, pp. 126–7.
40 *Said or Sung*, pp. 91–2.
41 *A Celebration of Faith*, p. 88.
42 *The Brink of Mystery*, p. 21.
43 *Interpretation and Belief*, p. 167.
44 *Faith and Logic*, p. 99.

10 CONTEMPORARY UNITARIANISM

1 I have in mind a number of Wiles' essays, collected together in *Working Papers in Doctrine* (SCM 1976) and *Explorations in Theology* 4 (SCM 1979) and his book *The Remaking of Christian Doctrine* (SCM 1974), and Lampe's essay 'The Essence of Christianity – IV. A Personal View' in *The Expository Times* for February 1976 and his Bampton Lectures, *God as Spirit* (OUP 1977).
2 L. Hodgson, *The Doctrine of the Trinity* (Nisbet 1943), p. 25.
3 *The Remaking of Christian Doctrine*, pp. 17ff.
4 *God as Spirit*, pp. 33 and 139.
5 'Perichoresis – Reflections on the Doctrine of the Trinity', *Theology*, July 1977; see above, chapter 2.
6 *Summa Theologiae*, Ia, 27–43. In the article mentioned in the previous note, I did not do justice to the 'psychological analogy'.
7 Mowbrays 1979. See especially chapter IV, where the difficulty of advancing from a binitarian to a trinitarian view is stressed.
8 *Summa Theologiae*, Ia, 31, 3 ad 1.
9 *Church Dogmatics*, III, 4, paragraph 54. Barth is following Hilary of Poiters' exegesis here (*De Trinitate*, Bk IV).

[10] *Love Alone: The Way of Revelation* (Burns and Oates 1968), p. 71.

[11] The books referred to in the concluding paragraph are David Jenkins, *The Contradiction of Christianity* (SCM 1976); C. F. D. Moule, *The Origins of Christology* (CUP 1977); G. C. Stead, *Divine Substance* (OUP 1977) and R. W. McKinney (ed.), *Creation, Christ and Culture* (T. & T. Clark 1976) for the essay by D. M. MacKinnon on 'The Relation of the Doctrines of the Incarnation and the Trinity'.

11 'TRUE' AND 'FALSE' IN CHRISTOLOGY

[1] John 16.6. The other references are 18.37, 8.31f. and 16.13f.

[2] W. Cantwell Smith, *Questions of Religious Truth* (Gollancz, 1967).

[3] See W. A. Christian, *Meaning and Truth in Religion* (Princeton University Press, 1964).

[4] D. Z. Phillips, *Faith and Philosophical Enquiry* (RKP, 1970).

[5] For example, A. Jeffner, *The Study of Religious Language* (SCM Press, 1972) and R. G. Swinburne, *The Coherence of Theism* (The Clarendon Press, 1977).

[6] Plato, *The Republic*, Bks V–VII.

[7] M. Heidegger, *Discourse on Thinking* (Eng. trans. Harper and Row, 1966).

[8] K. Jaspers, *Philosophy of Existence* (Eng. trans. Basil Blackwell, 1971).

[9] M. Dummett, *Truth and Other Enigmas* (Duckworth, 1978), p. 24.

[10] Nietzsche, *The Twilight of the Idols*. We may remind ourselves that Nietzsche once said that it was a definition of truth that anything said by a priest was false.

[11] Aristotle, *Metaphysics*, 1011b, 26ff.

[12] P. T. Geach, 'On Worshipping the Right God', in *God and the Soul* (RKP, 1969).

[13] See W. A. Christian, *Oppositions of Religious Doctrines* (Macmillan, 1972).

[14] 2 Corinthians 5.19.

[15] A. M. Farrer, 'Can Myth be Fact?', in *Interpretation and Belief* (SPCK, 1976).

12 FURTHER REFLECTIONS AND RESPONSES

[1] See M. Goulder and J. Hick, *Why Believe in God?* (SCM 1983).

[2] See D. Cupitt, *Taking Leave of God* (SCM 1980) and subsequent books.

[3] SCM 1968.
[4] 'Incarnation or Inspiration – a False Dichotomy?', *Theology*, July 1977.
[5] SPCK 1984.
[6] See chapter 9 above.
[7] Chapter 5.
[8] *The Divine Trinity* (Duckworth 1985).
[9] *The Roots of a Radical* (SCM 1980), ch. III.
[10] See p. 2 above.
[11] *The Roots of a Radical*, p. 60.
[12] *Saving Belief*, p. 75.
[13] See chapter 10 above.
[14] *Christians and Religious Pluralism* (SCM 1983).
[15] See, for example, R. Panikkar, *The Unknown Christ of Hinduism* (DLT 1968).
[16] In *The Epworth Review*, May 1980, pp. 101–3.
[17] Cornell University Press 1986.
[18] *The Logic of God Incarnate*, p. 183.
[19] See *ibid.*, p. 186. In its own context, this rejoinder to Wiles is entirely apt.
[20] The Bodley Head 1943. The book was retitled *Voyage to Venus* for its paperback edition (Pan Books 1953).
[21] See now J. D. Barrow and F. J. Tipler, *The Anthropic Cosmological Principle* (OUP 1986), ch. 9.
[22] E. L. Mascall, *Whatever Happened to the Human Mind?* (SPCK 1980), pp. 54f.
[23] See above, p. 118.
[24] See his earlier book, *Via Media* (Longmans 1956).
[25] 'Austin Farrer and the Paradox of Christology', *The Scottish Journal of Theology*, vol. 35, pp. 145–63.

Index

Index

98, 100, 102, 105–11, 120, 122f., 130, 149, 166
Hodgson, L., 15, 60, 62, 128, 130f.
Hoskyns, E., 73
Houlden, L., 33

Illingworth, J. R., 56
immanence, 50f., 70, 132ff., 158, 161, 166, 169
impassibility, 43, 162
infallibility, 86f., 105, 110
inspiration, 4f., 9, 17, 62, 64, 72, 118, 122, 134, 136, 156f., 165, 169f.

Jaspers, K., 142
Jenkins, D., 137
John, St., 29, 75, 122, 136, 139, 147, 152
John of Damascus, 12, 57
John Paul II, 87
Jüngel, E., 40, 42, 155

Kant, I., 141, 143
kenosis, 8, 30ff., 40, 43, 45f., 48, 55, 57f., 66–9, 75f., 158, 162, 164f.
Kierkegaard, S., 4, 8
Küng, H., 83–91, 103

Lampe, G. W. H., 18, 33f., 36, 61, 63, 77, 126–37, 160, 162–6
Leontius of Byzantium, 57
Lewis, C. S., 124, 168
liberation theology, 85, 111
Liddon, H. P., 56
Loisy, A. F., 89
Lonergan, B., 19, 103
love, 1, 5, 14f., 18ff., 21, 30, 32f., 35f., 39f., 42f., 47, 50f., 62, 64, 66, 68f., 72, 78, 99, 104, 115, 118f., 123, 126, 131ff., 135ff., 165f.
Luciani, A., 87

MacKinnon, D. M., 69, 137f.
Macquarrie, J., 56, 61
Manson, T. W., 73
Mascall, E. L., 61, 169
Matthews, W. R., 61
Moberly, R. C., 56

Modernism, 58, 63, 84, 89, 103, 127, 170
Moltmann, J., 16, 40ff., 98, 155
Montefiore, H. W., 61
Morris, T. V., 166ff.
Moule, C. F. D., 37, 73, 81f., 107, 132, 137
Mozely, J. K., 37, 59ff., 62
mysticism, 4, 51, 64, 148

Nestorianism, 54
Newman, J. H., 39
Nietzsche, F., 144
Nineham, D. E., 33f.

Otto, R., 136

Pannenberg, W., 100, 155
Paul, St., 17, 29, 75, 100, 111, 134, 150
Phillips, D. Z., 140
Pittenger, N., 2
Pius X, 89
Plato, 27, 99, 142
Pohier, J., 85
political theology, 44
prayer, 17, 19, 24, 44, 110, 136
Prestige, G. L., 12
providence, 34, 51, 71, 74, 113, 120f., 124, 151, 170
Pseudo-Cyril, 12

Quick, O. C., 30, 33, 59ff., 68, 75, 137

Race, A., 160f., 165
Rahner, K., 103, 160
Ramsey, I., 46f.
Ramsey, M., 33, 90
Rashdall, H., 58, 60, 127
Rawlinson, A. E. J., 60, 73
religions, other, 7, 12, 28, 49–52, 63f., 96, 110f., 116, 123, 136, 149, 154, 160ff., 165–8, 170f.
Relton, H. M., 57
resurrection, 24f., 35, 40, 74f., 91ff., 100, 105, 114, 171f.
revelation, 10, 13f., 23, 33, 34f., 53, 59, 64, 96, 99f., 102, 105, 107,

Index

109f., 116, 122, 128f., 133, 136, 152, 166

Robinson, J. A. T., 2, 61, 90, 158ff.

Sanday, W., 57
science, 2, 10, 47, 58
Schillebeeckx, E., 81, 85–90, 92, 103
Schoonenberg, P., 85
Smart, N., 3, 8, 28
Smith, W. C., 139
Sobrino, J., 85
Spinoza, B., 3
spirituality, 4, 12, 63, 104, 160
Stead, G. C., 69, 137
Sykes, S. W., 94

Taylor, V., 73
Temple, W., 57, 59f., 134
Thomas Aquinas, 131f., 134
Thornton, L., 58ff.
Tillich, P., 111
Torrance, T. F., 40f., 86, 137, 173
trinity, 11–20, 21, 24, 28, 30, 35f., 37, 39, 42f., 46, 53, 64f., 68f., 73, 78, 86, 98, 105, 107, 109, 112, 117ff., 126–38, 147f., 155, 158, 160, 163, 165f., 170

Troeltsch, E., 2, 13, 127
truth, 27, 44, 53, 60, 94, 96–101, 103, 105, 107, 109f., 124, 139–53
Tyrrell, G., 89

unitarianism, 62, 126–38

Vatican I, 101
Vatican II, 103, 106
Virgin Birth, the, 97, 123f.
von Balthasar, H. U., 16, 40, 135

Ward, K., 156ff., 161
Westcott, B. F., 56
Weston, F., 30, 57f.
Whitehead, A. N., 36, 58
Wiles, M. F., 2, 12ff., 15, 19, 34, 52, 61, 78, 82, 126–37, 160
Williams, H. A., 8f., 18
Wilson, M., 169f.
Wittgenstein, L., 144
worship, 38, 63f., 80, 110, 133
Wurm, Bishop, 90–3

Young, F., 33, 36